The River Barle north of Withypool (Stage 10)

THE TWO MOORS WAY
DEVON'S COAST TO COAST

Devon's Coast to Coast route combines the well-established Two Moors Way between Ivybridge and Lynmouth with the Erme–Plym Trail, starting (or finishing) at Wembury in the South Devon National Landscape, to give a 188km (117 mile) long-distance walk across England's southwest peninsula. The route crosses Dartmoor and Exmoor and gives the walker the chance to experience all that this rural county has to offer.

Contents and using this guide

This booklet of Ordnance Survey 1:25,000 Explorer® maps has been designed for convenient use on the trail and includes:

- a key to map pages (pages 2–3) showing where to find the maps for each stage.
- the full and up-to-date line of the trail.
- an extract from the OS Explorer map legend (pages 65–67).

In addition, the guidebook *The Two Moors Way* describes the route south to north from Wembury to Lynmouth (with outline description for walking the route in the opposite direction) and contains lots of other practical and historical information.

© Cicerone Press 2026

Second edition 2026

ISBN: 978 1 78631 318 8

First edition 2019

Photos © Sue Viccars

Cicerone's EU representative for GPSR compliance is Easy Access System Europe, Mustamäe tee 50, 10621 Tallinn, Estonia. Email gpsr.requests@easproject.com.

Two Moors Way

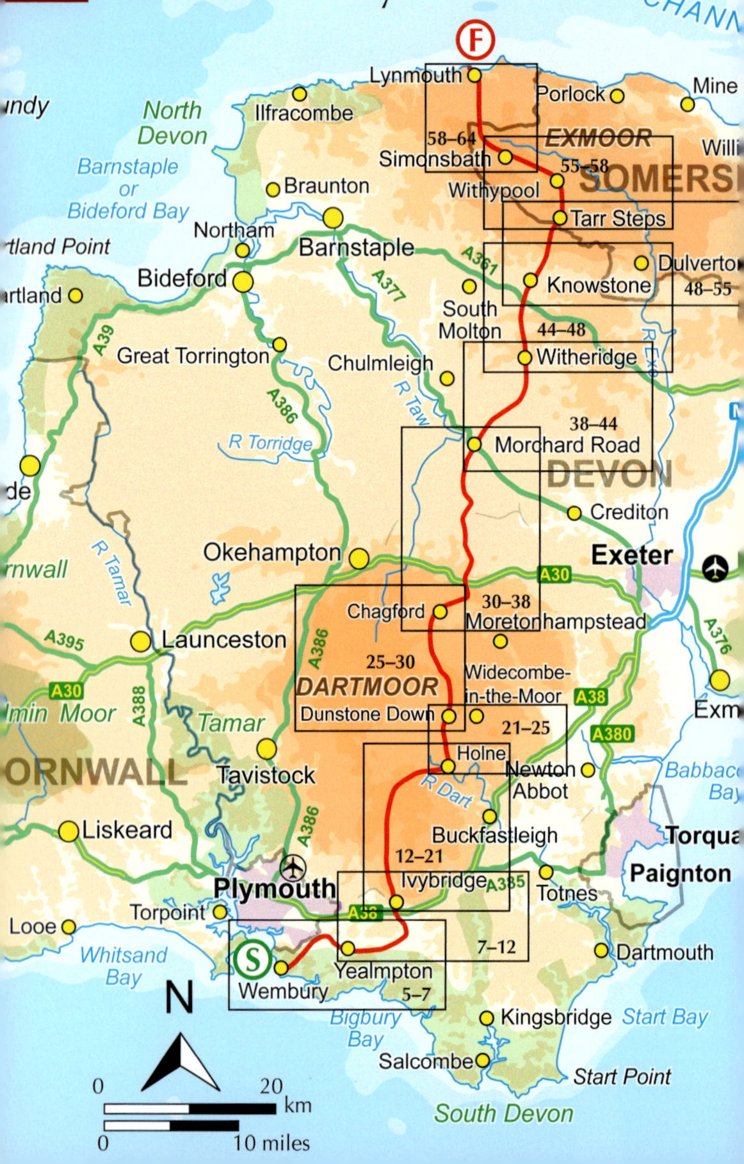

THE TWO MOORS WAY

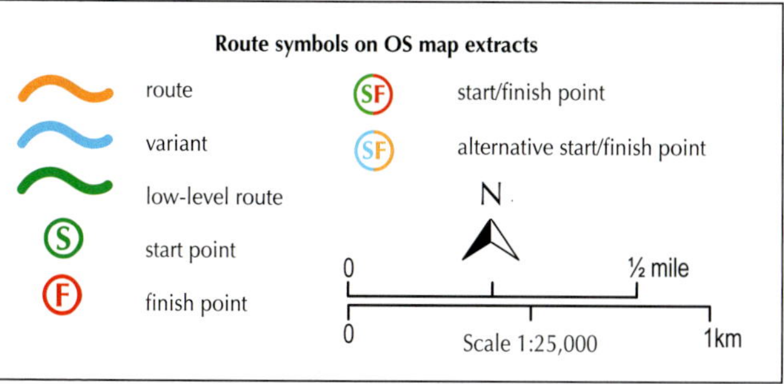

4
Dodovens Farm
Chittleburn Wood
Combe
Chittleburn Cross
Garden Centre
Fordbrook Farm
Cofflete
South Barton
Quarry (Stone)
Sterts Farm
FB
Wapplewell
Tor Hill Farm
Spriddlestone
NTL
Alberville
Halwell
Halwell Wood
Combe Wood
Trune Wood
Spriddlestone
Barton
Spriddlestone House
Andton Wood
Hollacombe Wood
Erme-Plym Trail
Coombe Farm
Higher Spriddlestone
Knapps Wood
Ridge Cross
Higher Leyford
Jew's Wood
Sch
Wembury Road
Cemy
Playing Field
Leyford Parks
Hollacombe
Staddiscombe
Higher Trune
Sch
Budds Wood
Radford Woods Nature Reserve
Basinghall Plantation
Courtgates
Manor Farm
Leyford Farm

Wembury Beach to Yealmpton
Start: Wembury Beach
Finish: Yealmpton
Distance: 12km (7.5 miles)
5
Raneleigh Farm
Park Wood
Spirewell
Traine Rd
Trescan
Park Wood
Brick Works
Quay
Steer Point
Hanaford Green
The Woodlands
Home Farm
Traine Farm
Langdon Court Hotel
West Wembury
Resr
Crawl Wood
Langdon Lodge
Ford Farm
PO
Knighton
Ford Wood
Sch
Hele Almshouses
Langdon Barton
Ford Road
Wembury House
South Wembury Wood
Quay
River Yealm
Shortaflete Creek
WEMBURY CP
Erme-Plym Trail
Churchwood Valley
Old Barton
Thorn
Quay
Newton Wood
South Barton Farm
Wembury
Ashey Plot
Sewage Works
Coleshill Brake
Marine Centre
Beacon Hill House
West Coast Path
Parson farm
Horsewells
Blackstone Rocks
High Cliffs
New Barton
Court Wood
Clitters Wood
Old Coastguard
Quay
Newton Ferrers
The Tomb
Ferries P (Summer)
Quays

6
Sch
Sherford Kilns (dis)
East Sherford Cross
SHERFORD
Spr
Hare
Fa
BRIXTON CP
74
80
West Sherford
Sherford Cotts
Sprs
Spr
43
101
69
60
Spr
89
H
A
53
Spr
Spr
2
Chittleburn Wood
Wollaton Cross
Wollaton
Wollaton Plantation
88
70
Stamps Hill
50
Spr
Dodovens Farm
55
81
Venn Quarry (dis)
Scotch
Plantatio
FB
20
Chittleburn Cross
Garden Centre
MS
Brixton
Silverbri
10
Fordbrook Farm
Combe
PO
Spr
52
Spr
Vic
Sch
Winston Hill Wood
NTL
Cofflete
Winston
Spr
Spr
58
Winston Plantation
Kitley (Hotel)
Little Quarry Plantation
Sewage Works
Fish
Plant
37
50
Dragberry Plantation
Quarry Plantation
Spr
51
40
Warren Wood
Spr
South Barton
Warren Point
Pars
P
Quarry (Stone)
Mudbank Lake
Broad Ooze
10
20
54
Western Park Wood Brick Works
55
56
30
W
Broompark Wood
Cofflete Creek
09
MHW
West Wood
Brusheshill Wood
Wrescom
22
MLW
50

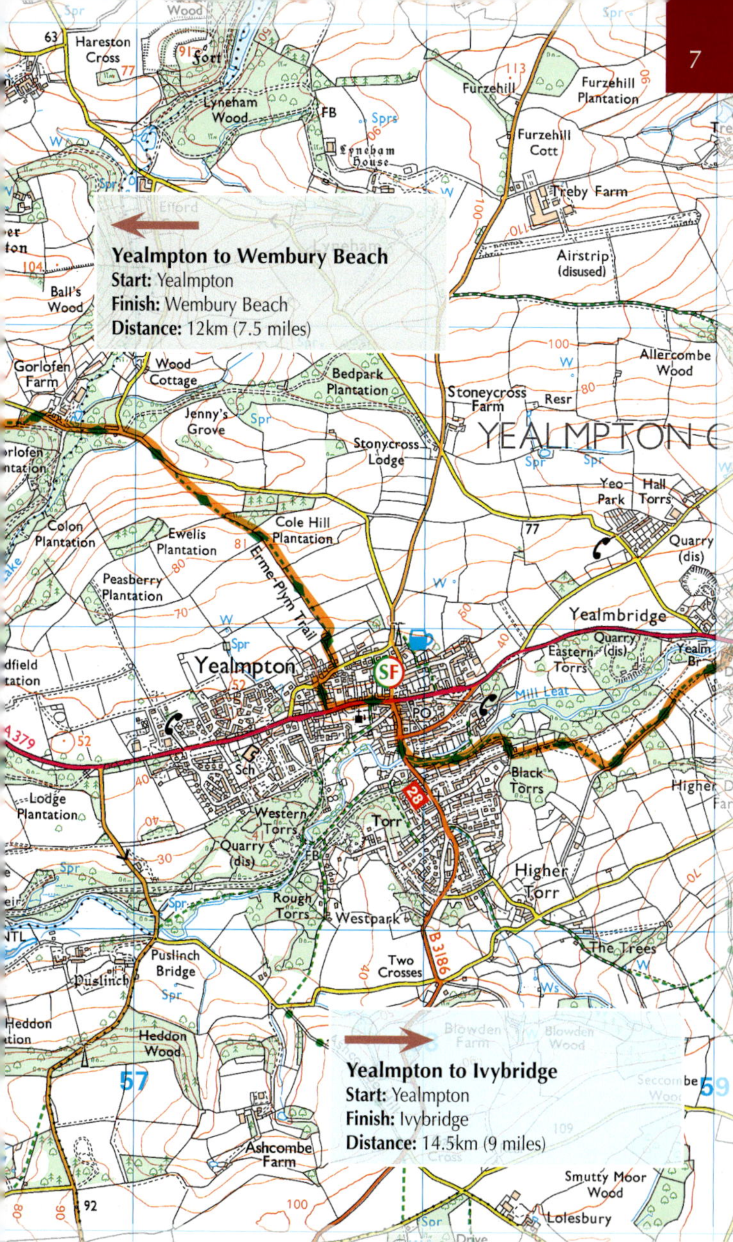

Yealmpton to Wembury Beach
Start: Yealmpton
Finish: Wembury Beach
Distance: 12km (7.5 miles)
Yealmpton to Ivybridge
Start: Yealmpton
Finish: Ivybridge
Distance: 14.5km (9 miles)
Hareston Cross
Lyneham Wood
Fort
FB
Lyneham House
Furzehill
Furzehill Plantation
Furzehill Cott
Treby Farm
Airstrip (disused)
Ball's Wood
Gorlofen Farm
Wood Cottage
Bedpark Plantation
Stoneycross Farm
Resr
Allercombe Wood
Jenny's Grove
Stonycross Lodge
YEALMPTON C
Orlofen Plantation
Colon Plantation
Ewelis Plantation
Cole Hill Plantation
Yeo Park
Hall Torrs
Peasberry Plantation
Erme-Plym Trail
Quarry (dis)
Yealmbridge
Quarry (dis)
Eastern Torrs
Yealm Br
Field ation
Yealmpton
SF
PO
Mill Leat
Black Torrs
Higher D Far
A379
Sch
Lodge Plantation
Western Torrs
Quarry (dis)
Torr
Higher Torr
The Trees
Rough Torrs
Westpark
B 3186
Puslinch Bridge
Two Crosses
Blowden Farm
Blowden Wood
Heddon ation
Heddon Wood
Seccombe Wood
Puslinch
57
59
Ashcombe Farm
Smutty Moor Wood
Lolesbury
92

Furzehill
Furzehill Plantation
Furzehill Cott
Treby Farm
Airstrip (disused)
Old Treby Farm
Treby Wood
Treby Ham
Lotherton Bridge
Oakhill Farm
Winsor Cross
Winsor
135
Yeo Quarry (dis)
Worston Mill
Worston
28
Allercombe Wood
Yeo Farm
Worston Wood
River Yealm
Stoneycross Farm
Resr
Quarry (dis)
Weir
YEALMPTON CP
Spr
Spr
Yeo Park
Hall Torrs
Orchard Farm
Longbrook Farm
23
77
Quarry (dis)
W
Yealmbridge
MS
37
Quarry (dis)
Eastern Torrs
Yealm Br
Depot
Mill Leat
Splatt
Erme
Black Torrs
Higher Dunstone Farm
Dunstone
118
Higher Torr
118
Hares Wood
105
109
The Trees
W
Ws
Crebar
Fursdon
Wonnell Barn
Blowden Farm
Blowden Wood
102
58
B 3186
Seccombe Wood
59
60
Gala Cross
Resr
109
110
Marland Cross
Smutty Moor Wood
Creacombe Solar Farm
Luson
Lolesbury
Spr
Drive
86
28
vo
sses

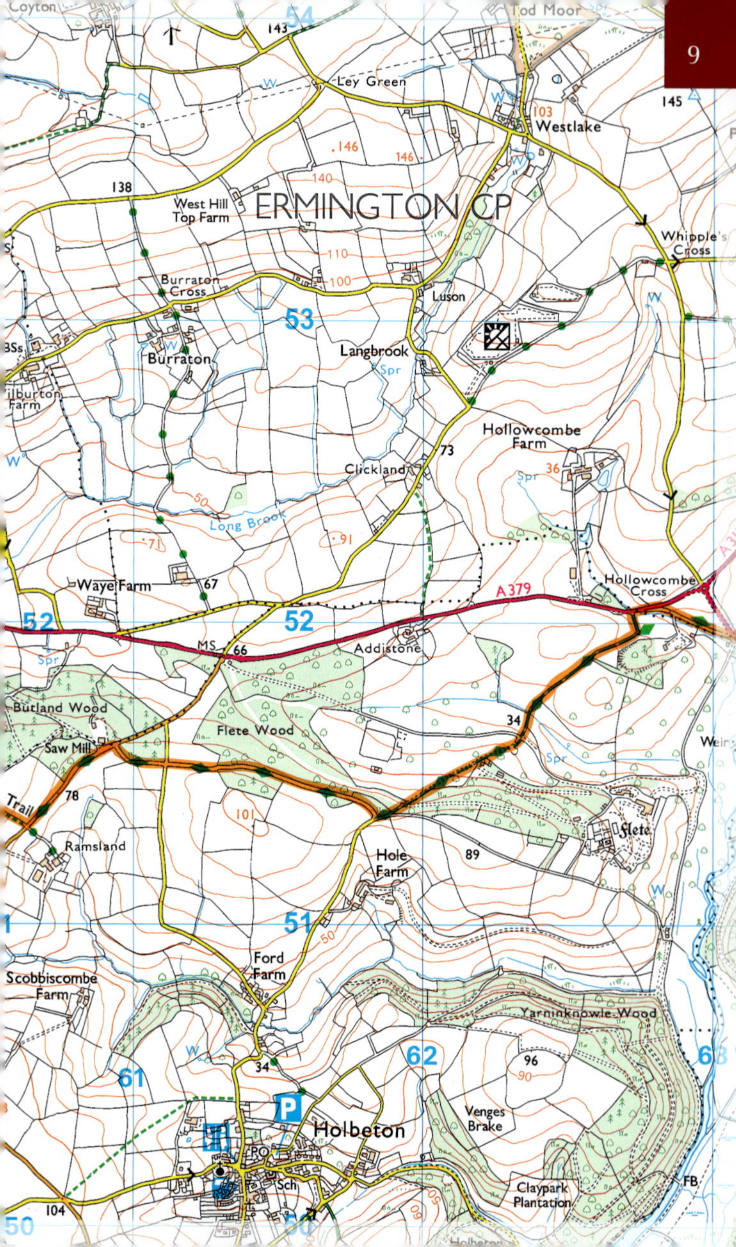

9
Coyton
Tod Moor
54
143
Ley Green
Westlake
103
145
146
146
140
138
West Hill Top Farm
ERMINGTON CP
110
Whipple's Cross
100
Burraton Cross
53
Luson
BSs
Langbrook
Spr
Burraton
Hollowcombe Farm
Tilburton Farm
Spr
36
Clickland
73
W
50
Long Brook
91
71
Waye Farm
67
A379
Hollowcombe Cross
52
52
Spr
MS
66
Addistone
A3
Butland Wood
Flete Wood
34
Weir
Saw Mill
Spr
Trail
78
Flete
101
Ramsland
Hole Farm
89
51
50
Ford Farm
Scobbiscombe Farm
Yarninknowle Wood
W
62
96
34
90
61
63
P
Venges Brake
Holbeton
PO
Sch
Claypark Plantation
FB
104
50
50
60

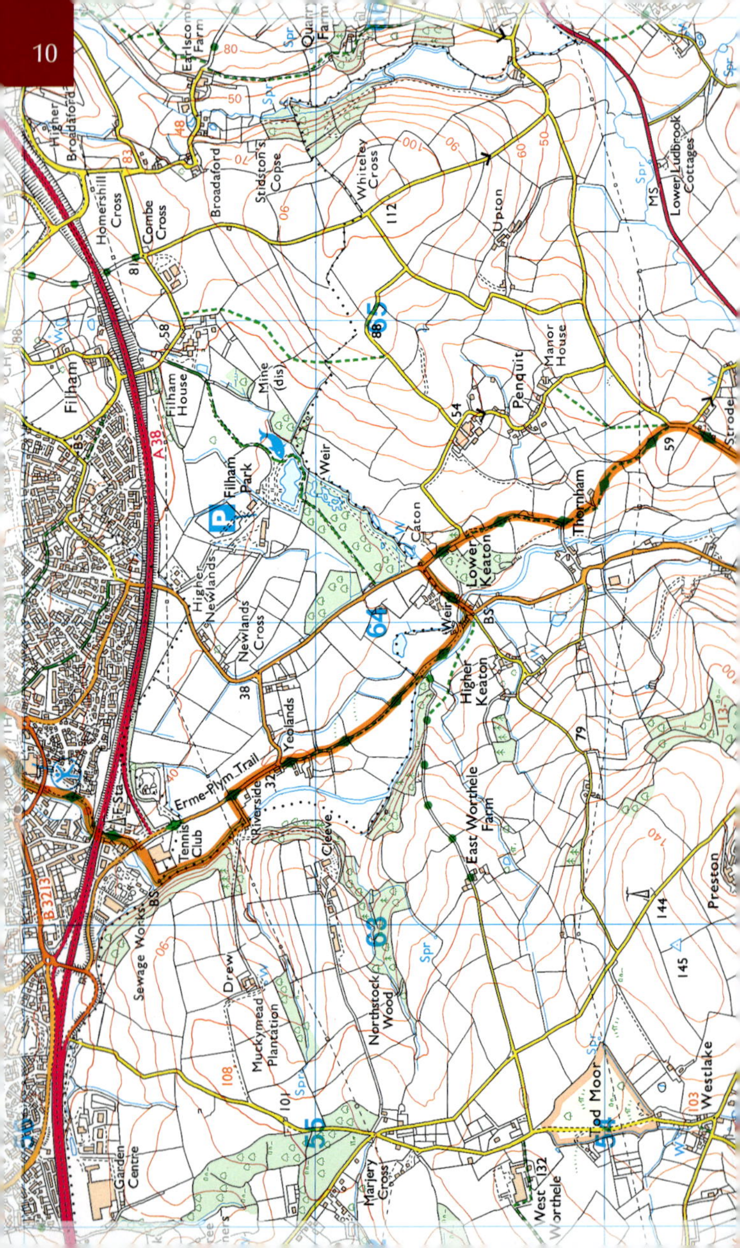

Earlscombe Farm
Quarry Farm
Whiteley Cross
Upton
Lower Ludbrook Cottages
Stidston's Copse
Broadaford
Higher Broadaford
Homershill Cross
Combe Cross
Filham
Filham House
Filham Park
Mine (dis)
Weir
Penquit
Manor House
Thornham
Strode
Caton
Lower Keaton
Higher Newlands
Newlands Cross
Weir
Higher Keaton
East Worthele Farm
Preston
Erme-Plym Trail
Yeolands
Riverside
Cleeve
Tennis Club
Sewage Works
Drew
Muckymead Plantation
Northstock Wood
West Worthele
Marjery Cross
Westlake
Moor
A38
B3213

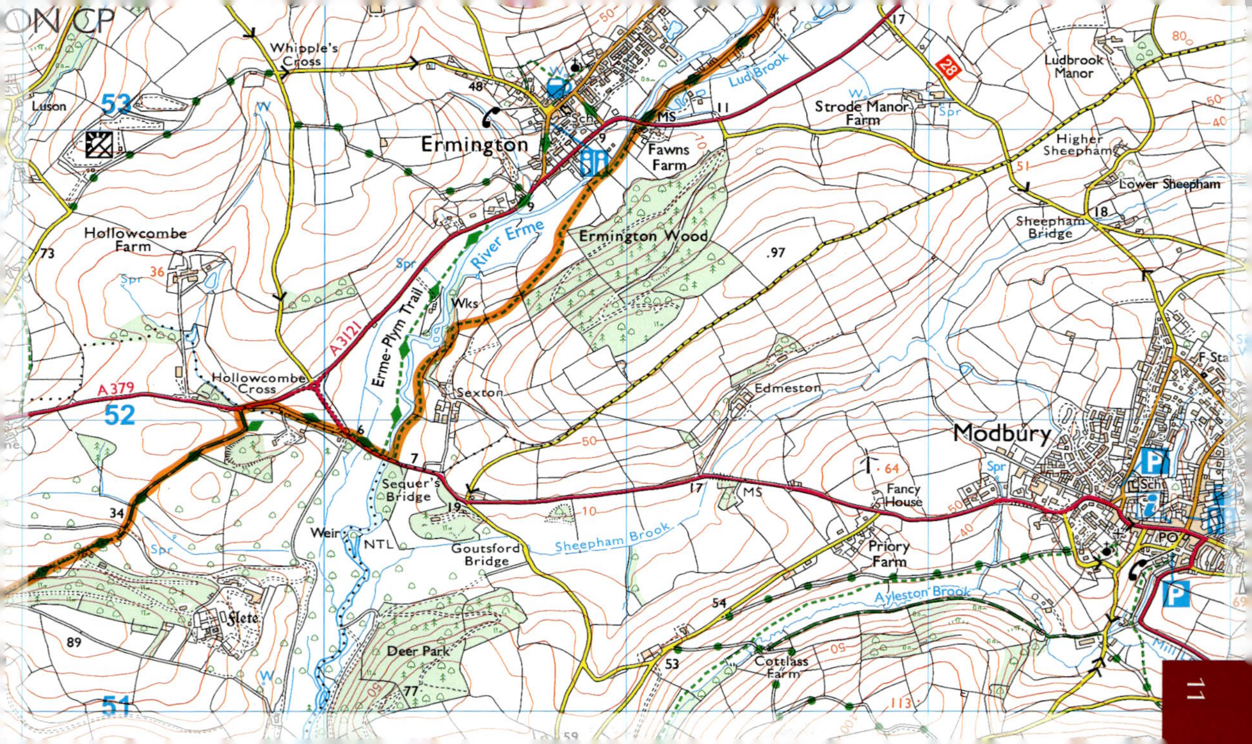

ON CP
Whipple's Cross
Ludbrook Manor
Lud Brook
80
28
Strode Manor Farm
50
40
Luson
53
Higher Sheepham
Ermington
48
Sch
MS
11
51
Fawns Farm
9
Lower Sheepham
Sheepham Bridge
18
Hollowcombe Farm
73
River Erme
Spr
Ermington Wood
.97
36
Spr
Wks
Erme-Plym Trail
A3121
Edmeston
A379
52
Hollowcombe Cross
Sexton
50
Modbury
64
6
7
17
MS
Fancy House
Spr
50
40
34
Sequer's Bridge
19
Sheepham Brook
Priory Farm
PO
Weir
NTL
Goutsford Bridge
10
54
Flete
89
Deer Park
53
Cottlass Farm
50
77
51
113
59
11

Ivybridge to Holne (high-level route)
Start: Ivybridge
Finish: Holne
Distance: 21.8km (13.5 miles)
Ivybridge to Yealmpton
Start: Ivybridge
Finish: Yealmpton
Distance: 14.5km (9 miles)
Weatherdon Hill
Cairns
Torlands Barn
Meads
FBs
Combeshead
East Combeshead
Combeshead
Enclosure
Homestead
Marker Stone
Cairn
Addicombe
Cairn
Quarry (disused)
Pithill Wood
Wood
FB
FBs
Lukesland
Lukesland Farm
Quarry (disused)
Pit-Hill Farm
River Erme
Erme Wood
Dartmoor Way
BS
Dartmoor Way
Two Moors Way
Ermewood
Dartmoor Way
Quarry (disused)
Quarries (disused)
Henlake Down
Weir
FB
Spr
Resr
Quarry (disused)
Earthwork
Stowford House
Rutt Farm
Quarry (dis)
RIDGE
Stowford Bridge
272
Rutt House
FB
Sch
Coll
Sch
IVYBRIDGE CP
Garfield
North Filham
P
2
MS
SF
TH
Sch
POR
CH
B 3213
Filham
Homersh Cross
Sta
Tennis Club
Erme-Plym Trail
High Newl
Newlands Cross
Riverside
Yeolands
Combe Cross
Mine
Weir

59
Eastern Beacon
Cairn
Butterdon
364 Hill
365)
Cairn
BSs
Long Barrow
Ivybridge to Holne (low-level route)
Start: Ivybridge
Finish: Holne
Distance: 26.8km (16.5 miles)
ongstone
(BS)
Enclosure
Burial Chamber
Cuckoo
Ball
Black
Pool
Wrangaton Golf Club
Deals
Brake
UGBOROUGH CP
Wrangaton Moor
Gate
Moorlands
225
162
230
CH Resr
58
Lud Brook
244
Torrs
Wood
Cross
Wrangaton
66
67
High Lane
W
210
Blackadon
Farm
Wrangaton
Business
Park
151
Western Beacon
Spr
Moorhaven
Village
Leigh Cross
139
Spr
West
Peeke
180
W
Cairn
ne Row
Spr
160
Monksmoor
2
140
128
57
Bittaford
MP
W
Forder
Quarry
(disused)
Underhill
Cantrell
Forder Brook
Forder Lane
edge
MS
Works
Ridge Road
Nine Milestone
Cross
Torpeek
Cross
Spr
MP
152
Hillhead
Cross
Whitehouse
Torpeek
140
Lutterburn
Lud Brook
W
Sch
Higher
Broadaford
111
148
Spr
Wood
Farm
Toby
Cross
Ugborough
97
MS
Bowcombe
Wood
130
Cemy
Spr
Quar
(disu
48
Earlscombe
Farm
50
80
Higher
Bowcombe
Haredon
Haredon
Cross
106
100
Waterman
Spr
Quarry
Farm
W
Spr

les Hill
Cairn
387
Cairn
Longstone
(recumbent)
Two Moors Way
Homestead
West Glaze R
Enclosure
334
Boundary
Work
Corringdon
Ball
High-level route
lements
Newland's
Brakes
65
Hobajons Cross
Cairns
66
Stone
Row
Glasscombe Ball
Cairn
67
Glaze Meet
Blowing house
(remains of)
Skitscombe
Wood
Corringdon
Wood
60
BS
Stone Row
Spurrell's Cross
Settlement
Scad Brook
Ford
Owley Moor
Gate
Cairns
358
Owley
Corner
Stone Row
BSs
Hangershell
Rock
Cairn
Beacon Plain
Beacon
Rocks
Hut Circle
Cist
Flat Stone
Hut Circles
378
59
Main Head Spr
Tumulus
Ugborough Beacon
eatherdon Hill
Eastern Beacon
Cairn
Cairns
350
Cairns
Cairns
Cairns
Creber's
Rock
350
Deals
Brake
Butterdon
364 Hill
(365)
BSs
Cairn
Long Barrow
300
260
UGBOR
Homestead
Marker Stone
Cairn
290
Longstone
(BS)
Enclosure
Burial Chamber
Cuckoo
Ball
Wrangaton Golf Club
Spr
230
Wrang
CH Resr
Black
Pool
Cairns
58
BSs
244
Torrs
Wood
320
BSs
334
Cairns
Western Beacon
Lud Brook
Leigh Lane
Blackadon
Farm
210
Spr
Moorhaven
Village
W
West
Peeke
Spr
Leigh Cross
Dartmoor Way
Stone Row
Cairn
160
Monksmoor
2
140
128
Quarry
(disused)
Bittaford

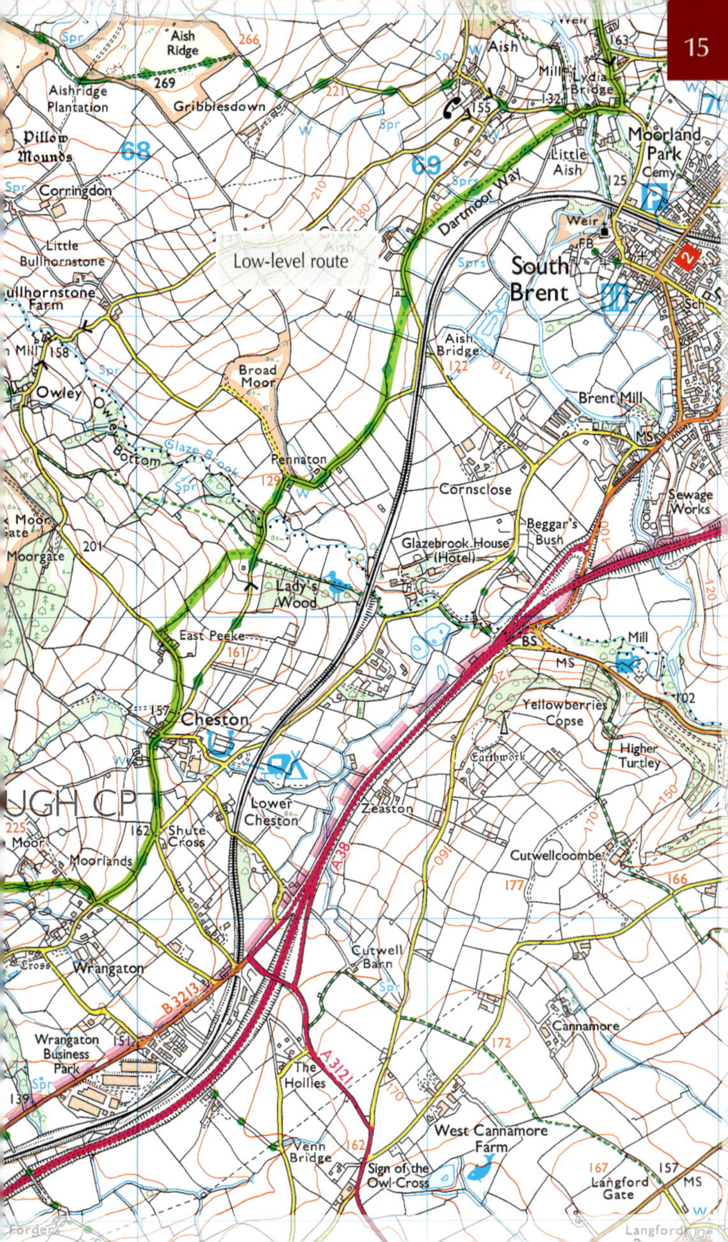
Aish Ridge
266
Aishridge Plantation
269
Gribblesdown
210
Pillow Mounds
68
69
Corringdon
Little Bullhornstone
Bullhornstone Farm
Mill 158
Low-level route
Owley
Owley Bottom
Glaze Brook
Broad Moor
Spr
Pennaton
129
Moor Gate
Moorgate
201
Lady's Wood
East Peeke
161
157
Cheston
UGH CP
225
Moor
Moorlands
162
Shute Cross
Lower Cheston
Wrangaton
B3213
Wrangaton Business Park
151
139
The Hollies
A3121
Venn Bridge
162
Sign of the Owl Cross
Weir
163
Aish
Mill
Lydia Bridge
132
155
Dartmoor Way
Little Aish
125
Moorland Park
Cemy
South Brent
Weir
FB
122
Aish Bridge
110
Cornsclose
Glazebrook House (Hotel)
Beggar's Bush
100
BS
MS
120
Brent Mill
MS
Sewage Works
Mill
102
Yellowberries Copse
Earthwork
Higher Turtley
150
Cutwellcoombe
177
166
Cutwell Barn
Spr
170
160
091
Cannamore
172
West Cannamore Farm
167
157
Langford Gate
MS
150
Langford
Forder
A38

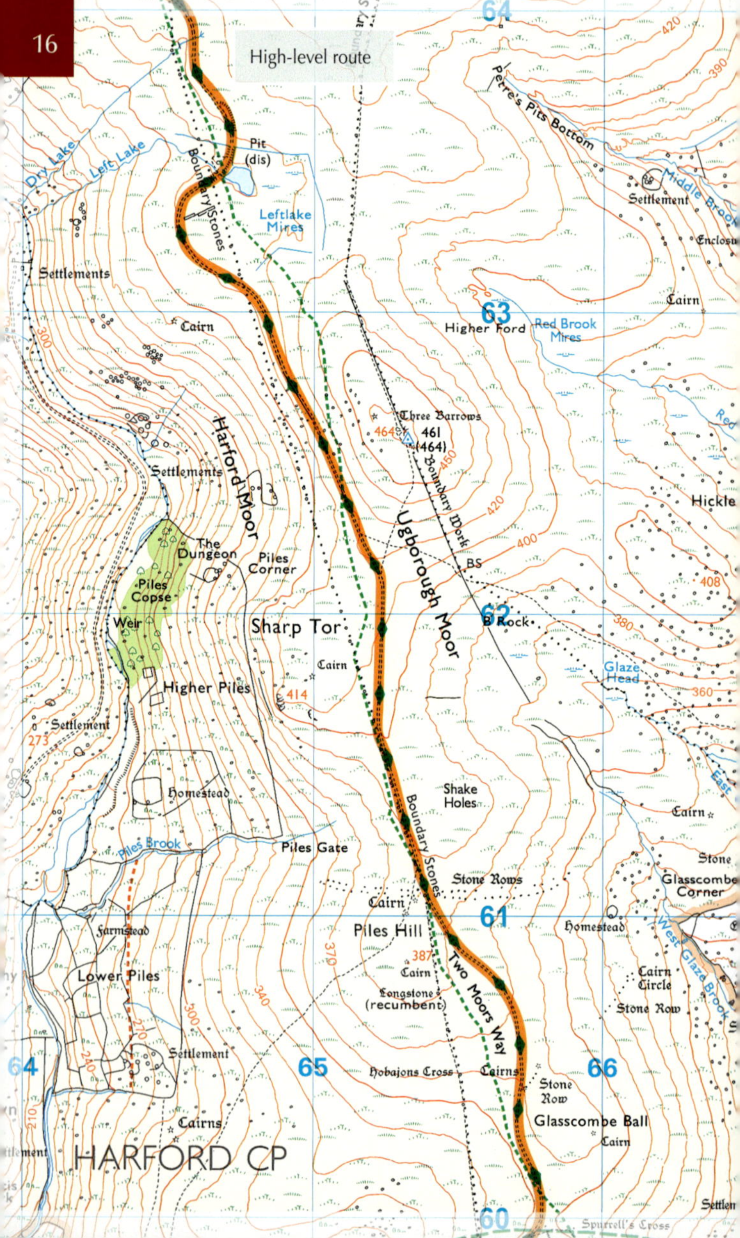

16
High-level route
64
63
62
61
60
64
65
66
Dry Lake
Left Lake
Settlements
Cairn
Settlements
Harford Moor
The Dungeon
Piles Corner
Piles Copse
Weir
Sharp Tor
Cairn
Higher Piles
414
Settlement
273
Homestead
Piles Brook
Piles Gate
Farmstead
Lower Piles
370
340
300
270
240
210
Settlement
Cairns
HARFORD CP
Boundary Stones
Pit (dis)
Leftlake Mires
300
Three Barrows
464
461
(464)
Ugborough Moor
Boundary Work
450
420
400
BS
B Rock
62
Shake Holes
Boundary Stones
Cairn
Piles Hill
387
Cairn
Longstone
(recumbent)
Hobajons Cross
Two Moors Way
Stone Rows
Cairns
Stone Row
Glasscombe Ball
Cairn
Spurrell's Cross
Petre's Pits Bottom
Settlement
Middle Brook
Enclosu
Cairn
Higher Ford
Red Brook Mires
Red
Hickle
408
380
Glaze Head
360
Cairn
Stone
Glasscombe Corner
Homestead
West Glaze Brook
East
Cairn Circle
Stone Row
Cairn
Settlen

Moor
System &
ement &
Cairns
Woolholes
Settlements
Dockwell Ridge
(dis)
Dockwell
Plantation
Dockwell
Farm
265
351
Low-level route
Hill
Black Tor
Cairns
Homestead
Yalland
Warren
270
Gisperdown
290
302
320
Settlements
Hunters
Stone
Shipley Tor
Shipley
Tor
Homestead
Yalland
Avon
Filtration
Station
Black Brake
P
Shipley
Bridge
Pillow
Mounds
Ford
233
Cattle Grid
240
221
Zeal
Cattle
Grid
Yalland Cross
Bala
Brook
210
Didworthy
Bottom
River Avon
218
Downstow Cross
Higher
Downstow
269
Spr
W
Spr
200
Lower
Downstow
Gingaford
272
SOUTH BRENT CP
62
Didworthy
Overbrent
204
Lower
Badworthy
Overbrent
Wood
Quarry
(dis)
Merrifield
Higher
Badworthy
190 171
Badworthy Brook
Spr
191
The
Plantation
220
216
Binnamore
Cross
Penstave
Copse
Ford
155
Lutton
Higher
Lutton
Treeland
250
Higher
Binnamore
203
Avon
Cott
Staddon
270
281
61
Spr
Weir
163
Spr
W
70
Spr
Aish
Ridge
266
Aish
Mill
Lydia
Bridge
Aishridge
Plantation
269
Gribblesdown
221
132
Spr
Moorland
Park
Cemy
Pillow
Mounds
68
Spr
W
Spr
155
Little
Aish
125
P
2
Corringdon
69
210
Dartmoor Way
Little
Bullhornstone
213
Great
Aish
180
Weir
FB
ullhornstone
Farm
Sprs
South
Brent
Sch

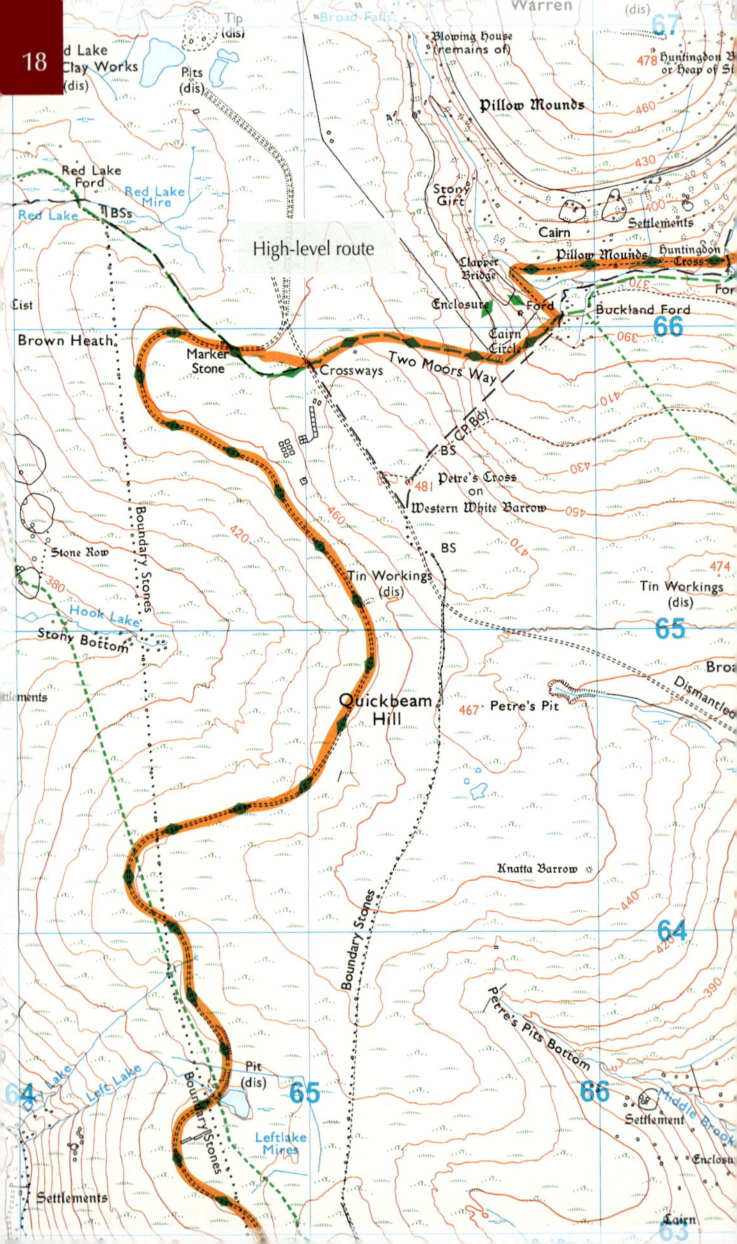

18
Warren
(dis)
67
Broad Falls
Tip
(dis)
Blowing House
(remains of)
478 Huntingdon
or Heap of St
Pillow Mounds
460
d Lake
Clay Works
(dis)
Pits
(dis)
430
Stony
Girt
400
Settlements
Cairn
Red Lake
Ford
Red Lake
Mire
High-level route
Pillow Mounds
Huntingdon
Cross
BSs
Red Lake
Clapper
Bridge
370
For
Enclosure
Ford
Buckland Ford
66
Cist
390
Brown Heath
Cairn
Circle
Marker
Stone
Crossways
Two Moors Way
410
CP Bdy
BS
430
Petre's Cross
on
Western White Barrow
450
420
460
BS
410
474
Tin Workings
(dis)
Stone Row
Tin Workings
(dis)
380
65
Hook Lake
Stony Bottom
Quickbeam
Hill
467 Petre's Pit
Broa
Dismantled
Boundary Stones
Knatta Barrow
440
64
420
390
Petre's Pits Bottom
Lake
Left Lake
Pit
(dis)
64
65
66
Boundary Stones
Settlement
Middle Brook
Leftlake
Mines
Enclosu
Settlements
Cairn
63

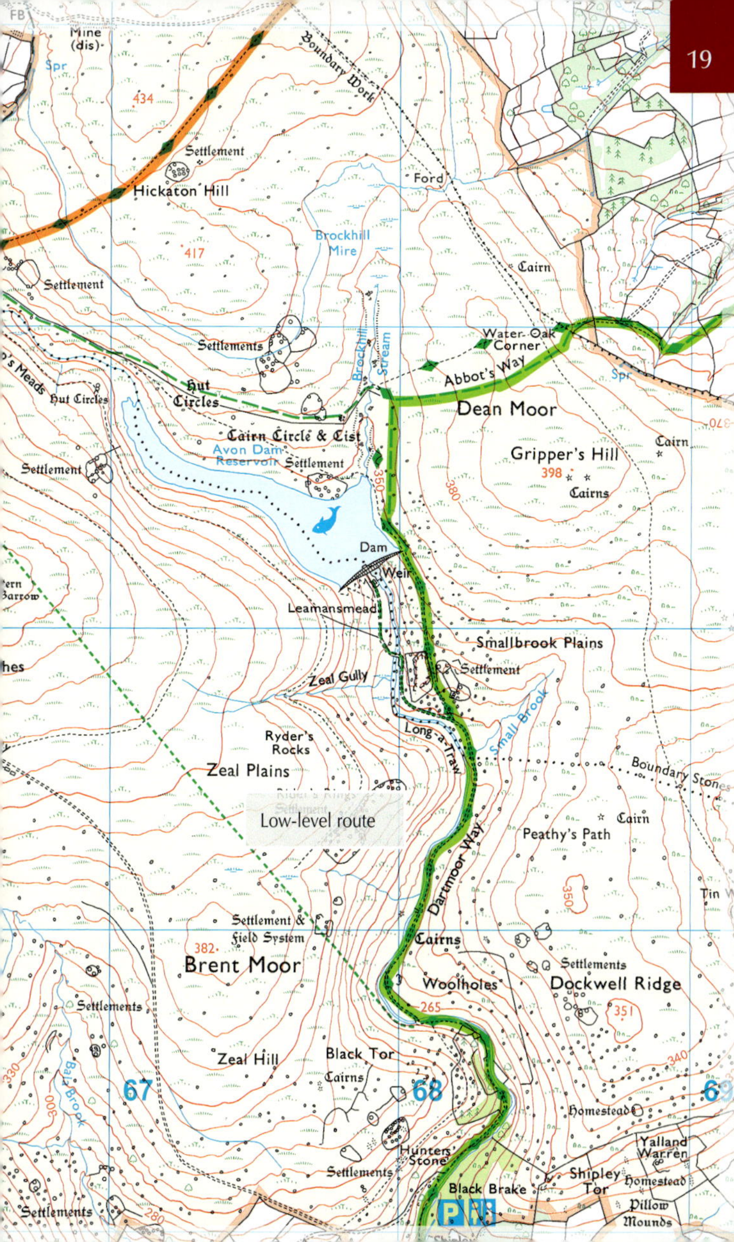

FB
Mine (dis)
Spr
434
Settlement
Hickaton Hill
417
Boundary Work
Brockhill Mire
Ford
Cairn
Settlement
Settlements
o's Meads
Hut Circles
Hut Circles
Water-Oak Corner
Abbot's Way
Spr
Dean Moor
370
Cairn Circle & Cist
Avon Dam Reservoir
Settlement
Brockhill Stream
Gripper's Hill
398
Cairns
Cairn
350
380
Settlement
Dam
Weir
tern Barrow
Leamansmead
Smallbrook Plains
Settlement
Zeal Gully
Long-a-Traw
Small Brook
hes
Ryder's Rocks
Zeal Plains
Boundary Stones
Ridon's Rings
Settlement
Low-level route
Cairn
Peathy's Path
Dartmoor Way
350
Tin W
Settlement & Field System
382
Brent Moor
Cairns
Woolholes
Dockwell Ridge
Settlements
265
351
Settlements
Zeal Hill
Black Tor
Cairns
340
Bala Brook
330
300
67
68
69
Homestead
Yalland Warren
Hunters Stone
Settlements
Shipley Tor
Homestead
Black Brake
Pillow Mounds
280
P

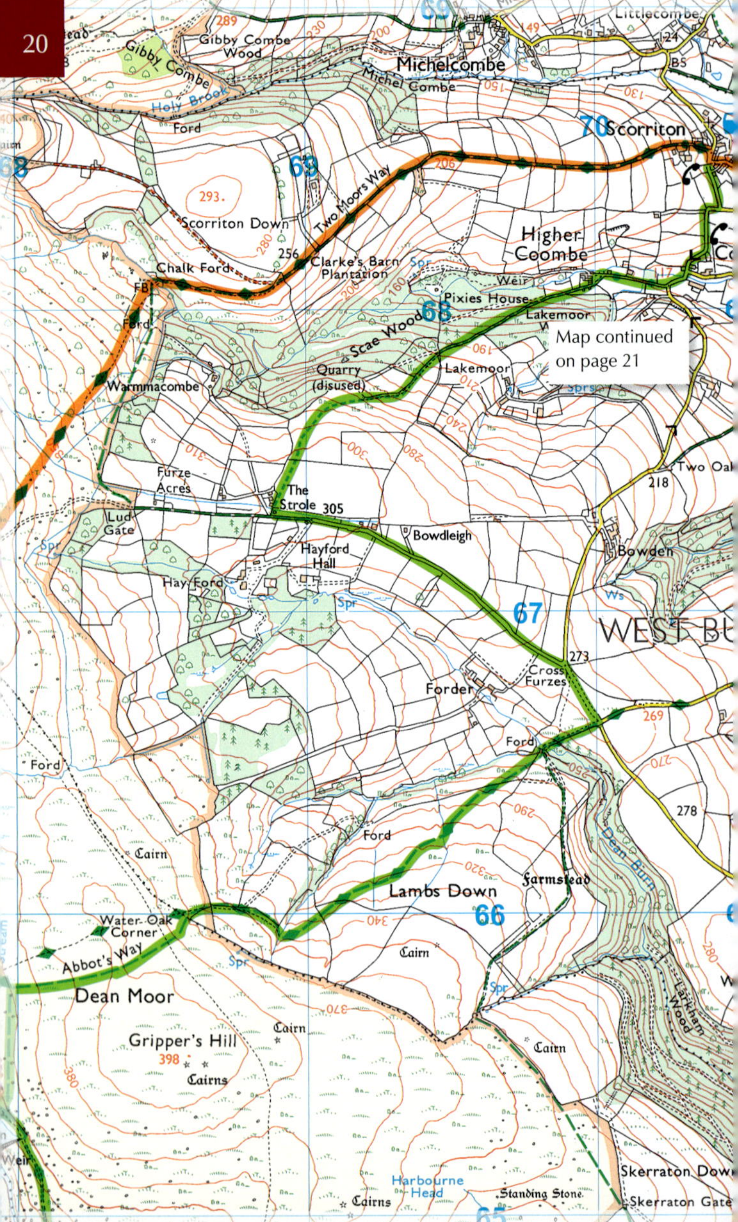
Gibby Combe Wood
Gibby Combe
Michelcombe
Michel Combe
Littlecombe
BS
Holy Brook
Ford
Scorriton
70
68
69
289
230
200
150
149
130
21
293.
Two Moors Way
206
Scorriton Down
280
256
Clarke's Barn Plantation
Higher Coombe
Chalk Ford
FB
Spr
Weir
Pixies House
160
Scae Wood
68
Lakemoor
190
Map continued on page 21
Ford
Warmmacombe
Quarry (disused)
Lakemoor
210
Sprs
218
Two Oak
240
310
Furze Acres
300
280
The Strole 305
Bowdleigh
Bowden
Lud Gate
Spr
Hayford Hall
Ws
Hay Ford
Spr
67
WEST BU
273
Cross Furzes
Forder
269
Ford
250
270
278
Dean Burn
Ford
290
Farmstead
Cairn
320
Lambs Down
66
Water Oak Corner
Abbot's Way
Spr
340
Cairn
Larkham Wood
Dean Moor
370
Spr
Gripper's Hill
398
Cairn
Cairns
380
Skerraton Dow
Weir
Harbourne Head
Standing Stone
Skerraton Gate
Cairns
65

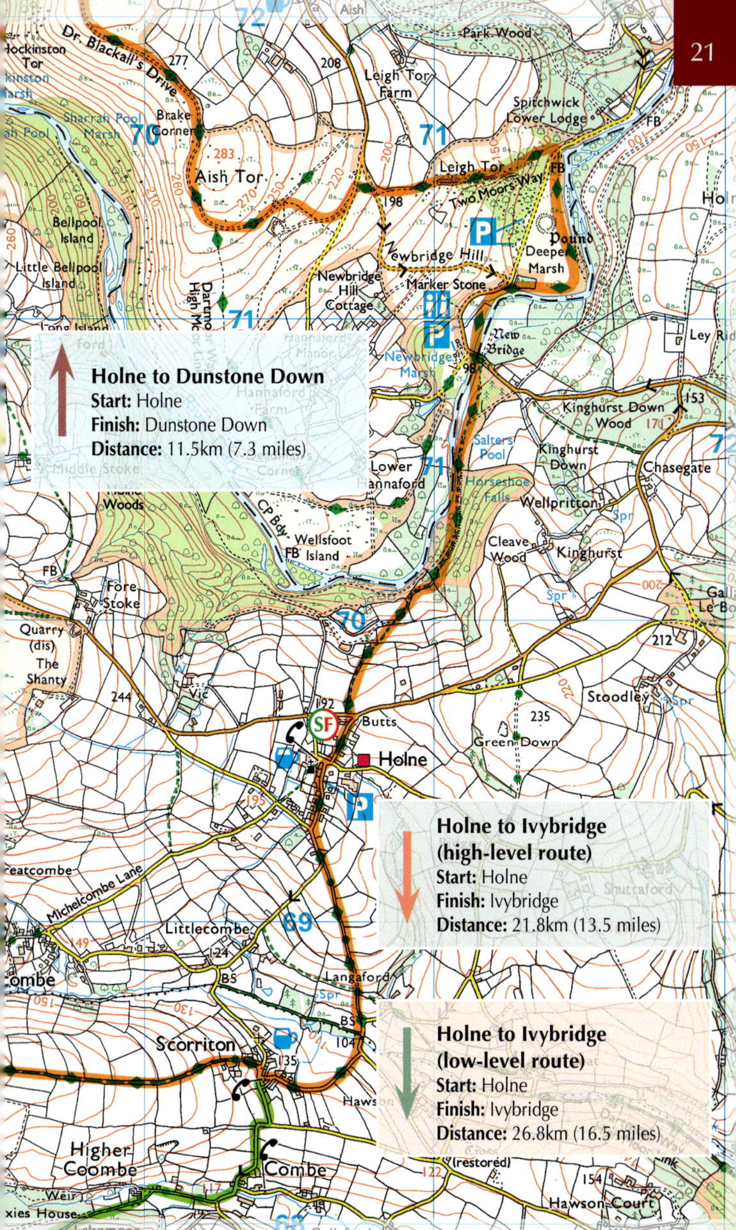

Dr Blackall's Drive
Park Wood
Leigh Tor Farm
Spitchwick Lower Lodge
FB
Hockinston Tor
Hockinston Marsh
Sharrah Pool Marsh
rah Pool
Brake Corner
Aish Tor
Leigh Tor
Two Moors Way
Pound
Deeper Marsh
Holn
Bellpool Island
Little Bellpool Island
Long Island
Dartmoor High Moor Link
Newbridge Hill
Newbridge Hill Cottage
Marker Stone
New Bridge
Ley Rid
Holne to Dunstone Down
Start: Holne
Finish: Dunstone Down
Distance: 11.5km (7.3 miles)
Middle Stoke
Hannaford Manor
Hannaford Farm
Newbridge Marsh
Kinghurst Down Wood
153
171
Holne Woods
CP Bdy
Corner
Lower Hannaford
Salters Pool
Horseshoe Falls
Kinghurst Down
Wellpritton
Chasegate
Spr
FB
Wellsfoot Island
Cleave Wood
Kinghurst
Spr
FB
Fore Stoke
200
Gal Le Bo
Quarry (dis)
The Shanty
212
244
Vic
192
Stoodley
Spr
SF
Butts
Holne
235
Green Down
Holne to Ivybridge
(high-level route)
Start: Holne
Finish: Ivybridge
Distance: 21.8km (13.5 miles)
195
Shuttaford
reatcombe
Michelcombe Lane
Littlecombe
149
24
Langaford
Spr
BS
Holne to Ivybridge
(low-level route)
Start: Holne
Finish: Ivybridge
Distance: 26.8km (16.5 miles)
ombe
BS
104
Scorriton
35
Haws
Higher Coombe
Combe
Weir
xies House
117
122
(restored)
154
Hawson Court
Lakemoor
Cullaford

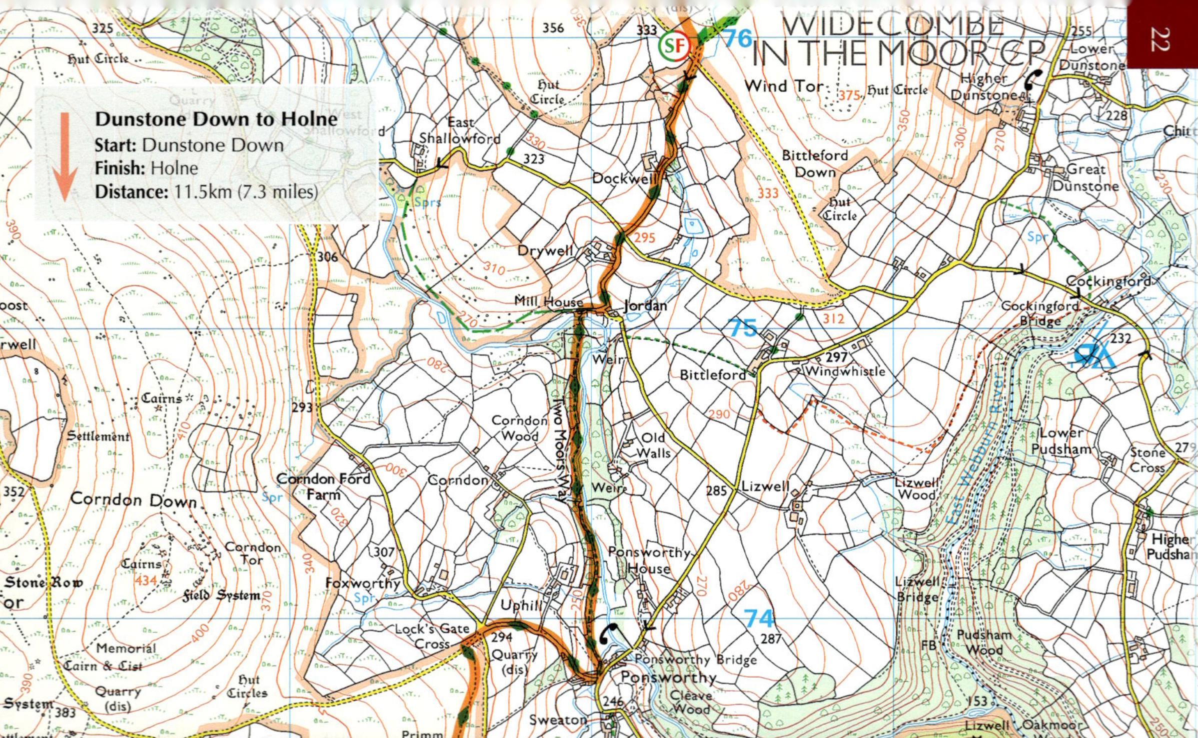

WIDECOMBE IN THE MOOR CP
76
Wind Tor
Hut Circle
Hut Circle
Higher Dunstone
Lower Dunstone
Chittlef
228
Great Dunstone
230
Bittleford Down
Hut Circle
Spr
Cockingford
Cockingford Bridge
232
75
312
297
Windwhistle
Bittleford
290
Lizwell
285
Lizwell Wood
Lizwell Bridge
Lower Pudsham
Stone Cross
279
Higher Pudsham
74
287
FB
Pudsham Wood
East Webburn River
153
Lizwell Oakmoor
250
325
356
333
East Shallowford
West Shallowford
330
323
Dockwell
333
295
Drywell
310
306
270
Mill House
Jordan
Weir
Two Moors Way
Old Walls
Weir
Corndon Wood
280
293
Corndon
Corndon Ford Farm
300
320
307
Foxworthy
Spr
Uphill
250
270
280
Ponsworthy House
Lock's Gate Cross
294
Quarry (dis)
Ponsworthy Bridge
Ponsworthy
246
Cleave Wood
Sweaton
Primm
Roost
Sherwell
Cairns
Settlement
410
352
Corndon Down
Spr
340
Corndon Tor
Cairns
434
Field System
370
Stone Row Tor
390
400
Memorial Cairn & List
Quarry (dis)
Hut Circles
Field System
383
Settlement

Dunstone Down to Holne
Start: Dunstone Down
Finish: Holne
Distance: 11.5km (7.3 miles)

River Webburn
North Wood
Town Wood
Blackadon Down
Blackadon Tor
Logwell Rock
Leusdon
Leusdon House
Leusdon Common
Lower Town
Spitchwick
The Glen
Great Lot Wood
Mistresses Piece
Buckland Bridge
Holne
Pound
Deeper Marsh
Great Wood
Park Wood
Spitchwick Manor
Spitchwick Lower Lodge
Spitchwick Farm
Works
Poundsgate
Lower Aish
Leigh Tor Farm
Leigh Tor
Two Moors Way
Newbridge Hill
Marker Stone
Newbridge
Higher Lodge
Tel Ex
Lake
Aish Tor
Dart High
Uppacott
Uppacott Farm
Lower Tor
Higher Tor
Hut Circles
Bel Tor
Logan Stone
Rock Basin
Bel Tor Corner
Mel Tor
Two Moors Way
Dr. Blackall's Drive
Brake Corner
Hockinston Tor
Meltor Wood
Sharrah Pool Marsh
Sharrah Pool
Hockinston Marsh
Bellpool Island
Little Bellpool Island
West Stoke Farm
Sherberton Common
Ollsbrim
Hut Circles
Sharp Tor
Dartmoor Way
High Moor Link
Rowbrook House
Broadstone
Rowbrook
Luckey Tor
White Wood
Dart Valley Nature Reserve
Bench Tor
Venford Brook
Blackpool
Water Works
Cattle Grid
Dam
Holne Moor Leat
Simons Lake
Hut Circles
Cross
Sturmstead

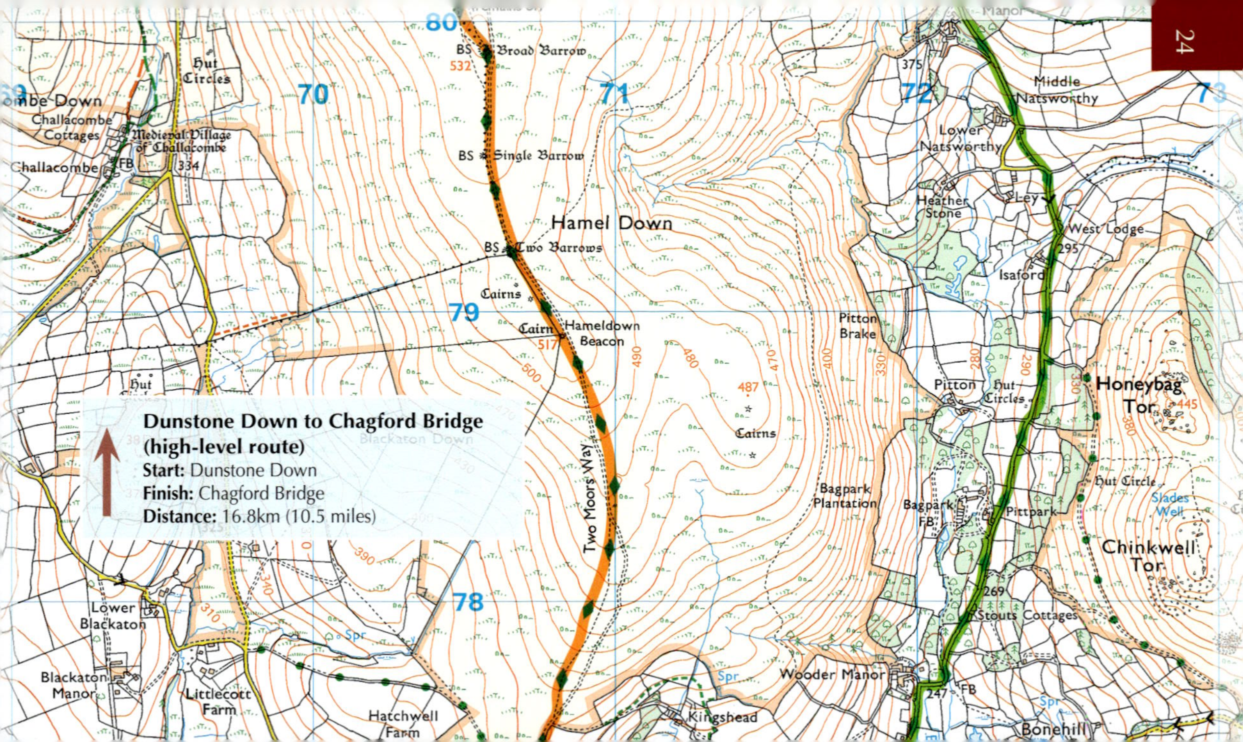

Hut Circles
ombe Down
Challacombe Cottages
Medieval Village of Challacombe
Challacombe
FB
334
70
80
BS Broad Barrow
532
BS Single Barrow
71
Hamel Down
BS Two Barrows
Cairns
79
Cairn Hameldown Beacon
517
500
490
480
487
Cairns
470
400
330
280
290
330
375
72
73
Middle Natsworthy
Lower Natsworthy
Heather Stone
Ley
West Lodge
295
Isaford
Pitton Brake
Pitton Hut Circles
Honeybag Tor
445
380
Hut Circle
Slades Well
Chinkwell Tor
269
Stouts Cottages
Bonehill
Bagpark Plantation
Bagpark FB
Pittpark
247 FB
Spr
Wooder Manor
Kingshead
Spr
Hut
Two Moors Way
Hut
Lower Blackaton
310
Spr
390
340
78
Blackaton Manor
Littlecott Farm
Hatchwell Farm
Blackaton Down
430

Dunstone Down to Chagford Bridge
(high-level route)
Start: Dunstone Down
Finish: Chagford Bridge
Distance: 16.8km (10.5 miles)

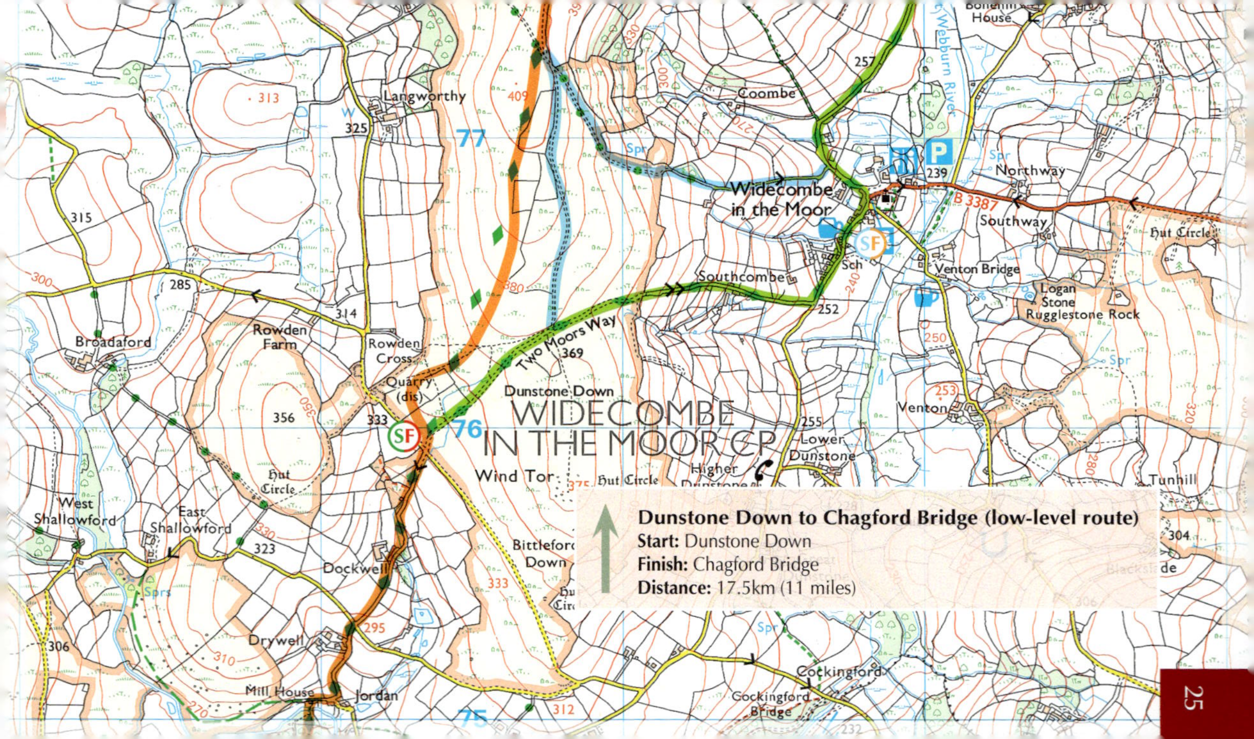

Bonehill House
Webburn River
313
Langworthy
325
77
409
330
Coombe
257
270
Spr
239
P
Northway
Widecombe in the Moor
B 3387
Southway
Hut Circle
315
SF
Sch
Venton Bridge
Logan Stone
Rugglestone Rock
300
285
314
380
Southcombe
252
240
250
Broadaford
Rowden Farm
Rowden Cross
Two Moors Way
369
Dunstone Down
WIDECOMBE
IN THE MOOR CP
255
Lower Dunstone
253
Venton
280
320
356
350
Quarry (dis)
333
SF
76
Wind Tor
375
Hut Circle
Higher Dunstone
West Shallowford
East Shallowford
Hut Circle
323
330
Dockwell
Bittleford Down
333
304
de
Sprs
306
310
295
Drywell
Mill House
Jordan
270
75
312
Cockingford
Cockingford Bridge
232
Spr
306

Dunstone Down to Chagford Bridge (low-level route)
Start: Dunstone Down
Finish: Chagford Bridge
Distance: 17.5km (11 miles)

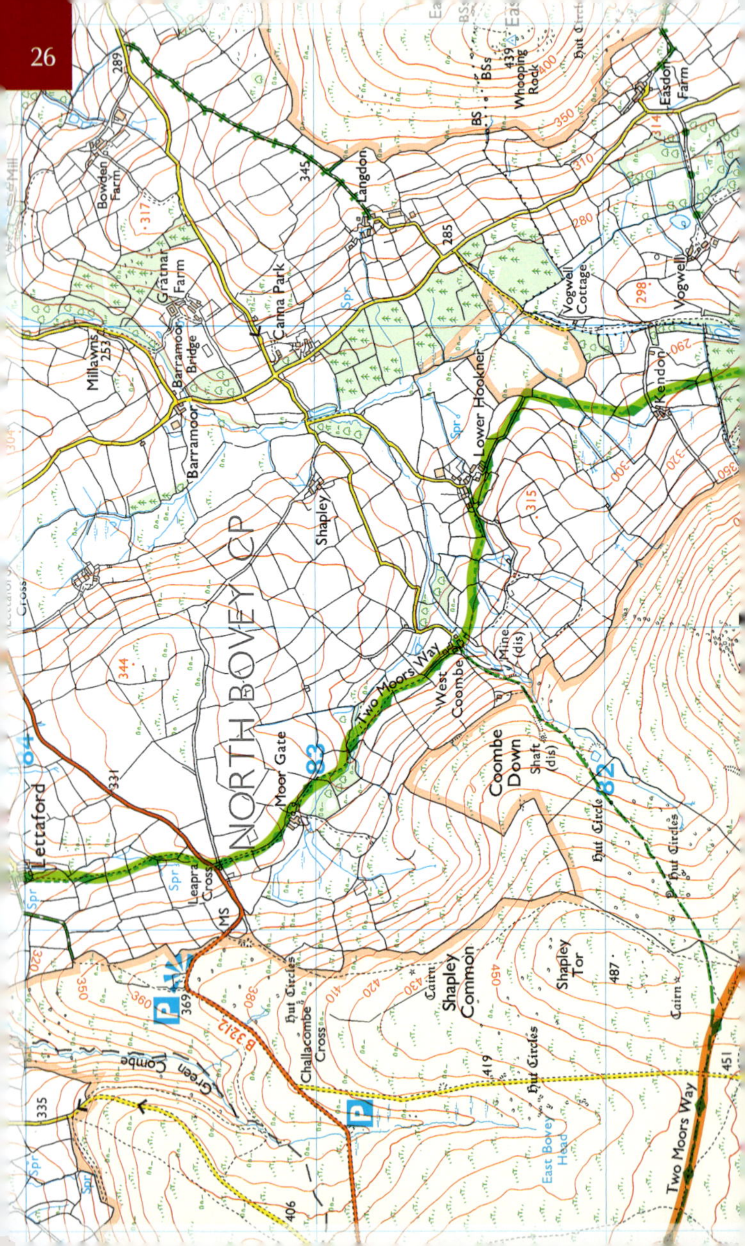
Bowden Farm
Gratnar Farm
Canna Park
Langdon
Whooping Rock
Easdon Farm
Vogwell Cottage
Vogwell
Kendon
Lower Hookner
Millawns
Barramoor Bridge
Barramoor
Shapley
NORTH BOVEY CP
Moor Gate
Two Moors Way
West Coombe
Mine (dis)
Coombe Down
Shaft (dis)
Hut Circle
Hut Circles
Lettaford
Leapra Cross
Shapley Common
Shapley Tor
Cairn
Challacombe Cross
Hut Circles
Green Combe
East Bovey Head
Two Moors Way
MS
Spr
B3212

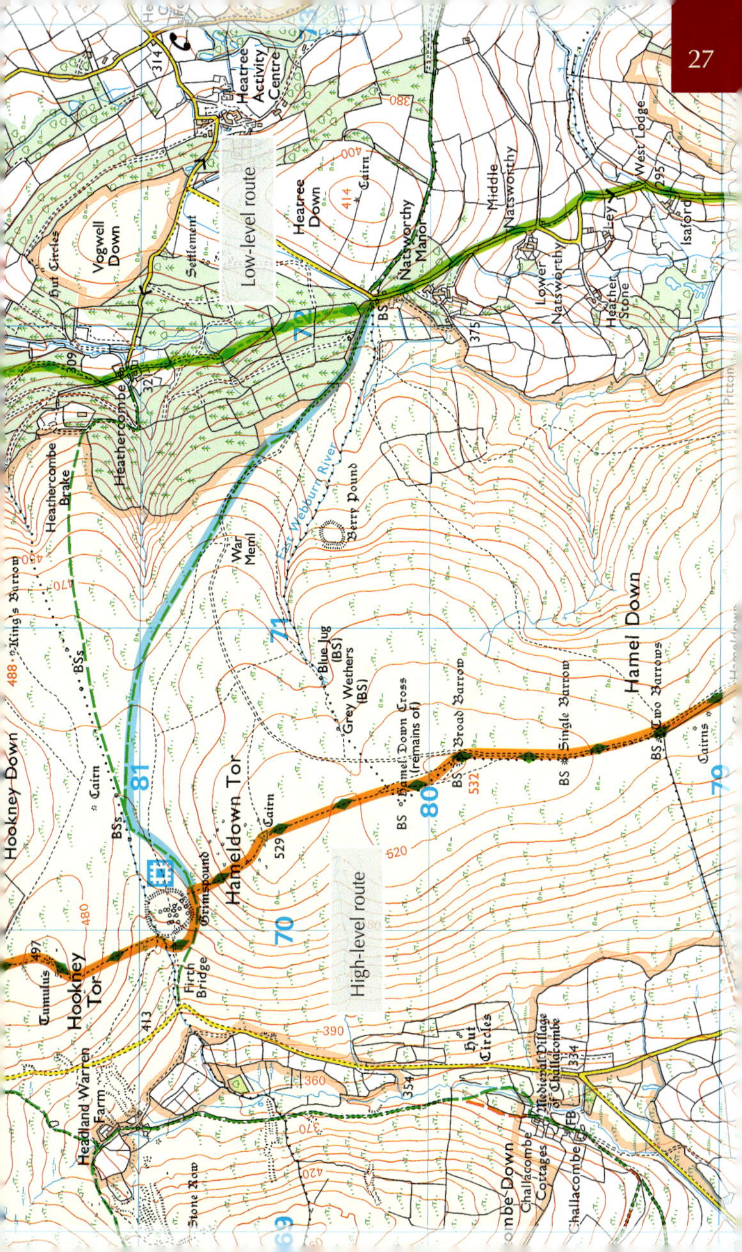
Heatree Activity Centre
314
Heatree Down
Cairn
414
400
380
Settlement
Vogwell Down
Hut Circles
309
Heathercombe
32
Heathercombe Brake
King's Barrow
488
BSs
430
470
Hookney Down
Cairn
BSs
81
Firth Bridge
Grimspound
Tumulus
497
Hookney Tor
480
413
Headland Warren Farm
Stone Row
420
370
360
390
354
334
Low-level route
High-level route
War Meml
East Webburn River
Berry Pound
71
Blue Jug (BS)
Grey Wethers (BS)
Hameldown Tor
Cairn
529
70
520
Hamel Down Cross (remains of)
BS
BS
80
532
Broad Barrow
Single Barrow
BS
Two Barrows
BS
Cairns
Hamel Down
79
Natsworthy Manor
BS
375
Middle Natsworthy
380
295
West Lodge
Ley
Isaford
Lower Natsworthy
Heather Stone
Pitton
Hut Circles
Challacombe Down
Medieval Village of Challacombe
Challacombe Cottages
FB
69

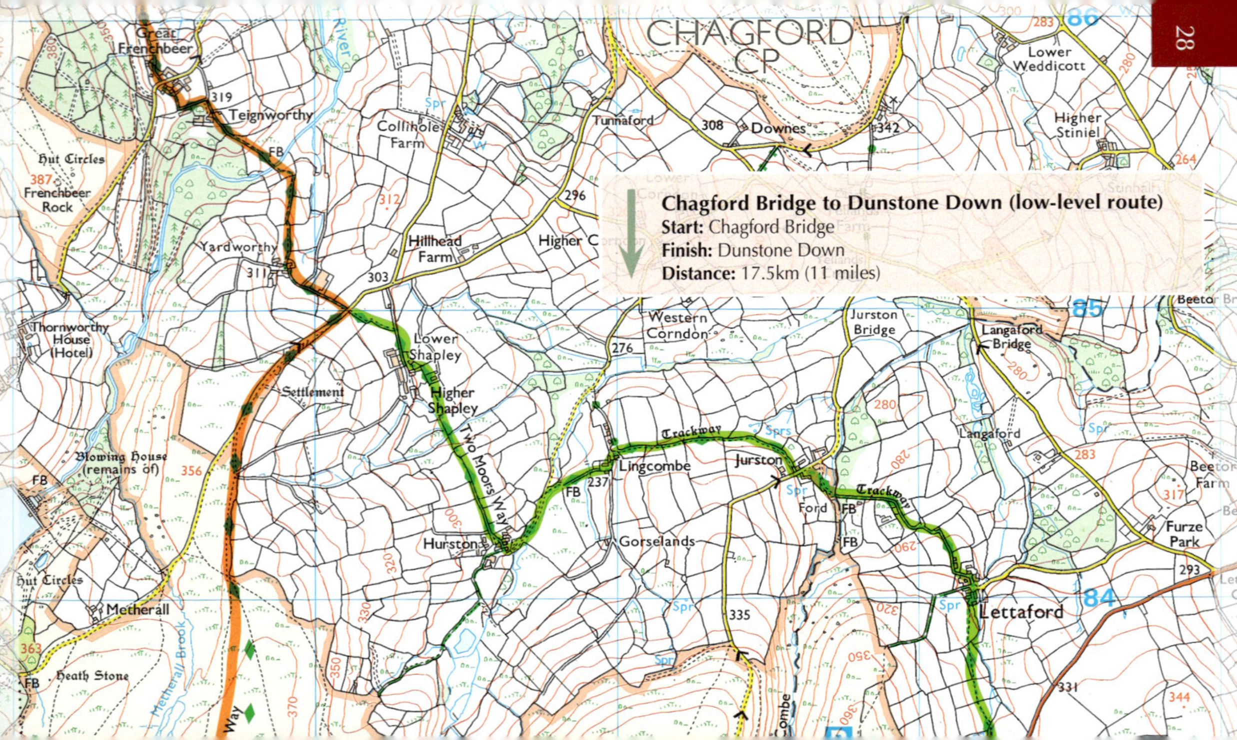

CHAGFORD CP
Chagford Bridge to Dunstone Down (low-level route)
Start: Chagford Bridge
Finish: Dunstone Down
Distance: 17.5km (11 miles)
Great Frenchbeer
Teignworthy
Collihole Farm
Tunnaford
Downes
Lower Weddicott
Higher Stiniel
Hut Circles
Frenchbeer Rock
Yardworthy
Hillhead Farm
Higher C
Thornworthy House (Hotel)
Lower Shapley
Higher Shapley
Settlement
Western Corndon
Jurston Bridge
Langaford Bridge
Langaford
Beetor Br
Two Moors Way
Trackway
Lingcombe
Jurston
Trackway
Blowing House (remains of)
FB
Gorselands
Ford
FB
FB
Spr
Beetor Farm
Furze Park
Hut Circles
Metherall
Hurston
Lettaford
Heath Stone
FB
Way
Combe
River
Spr
Sprs
Spr
319
387
311
303
312
296
276
237
300
320
330
350
356
363
370
335
290
320
350
360
331
344
293
317
283
280
264
342
308

NORTH BOVE
Moor Gate
Leapra Cross
MS
Green
B3212
369
380
370
Two Moors Way
West Coombe
Mine (dis)
Coombe Down
Shaft (dis)
King
King's
488
BSs
Hookney Down
Cairn
480
81
82
71
Low-level route
Challacombe Cross
Hut Circles
410
420
430
Cairn
450
Shapley Common
419
Hut Circles
East Bovey Head
Shapley Tor
487
Cairn
70
497
Tumulus
Hookney Tor
Headland Warren Farm
Cairn
413
451
Two Moors Way
P
406
BS
BS
MS
419
Hut Circles
Hut Circles
Clithers
Lakeland
The Hut
Ford
390
420
Hut Circles
460
69
Tumulus
487
Birch Tor
480
Headland Warren
High-level route
Chagford Common
Mine (dis)
Walla Brook
Cairn
400
Standing Stone
Stone Row
Hut Circles
Hut Circles
Bush Down
Bushdown Mine (disused)
68
BSs
Bennett's Cross
435
P
BS
MS
Two Moors Way
380
390
Two Moors Way
Shaft (dis)
378
Headland Warren
P
438
BS
427
King's Oven
Water Hill
Cairn
489
Hurston Ridge
67
470
FB: Vitifer Mine Leat
Warren House

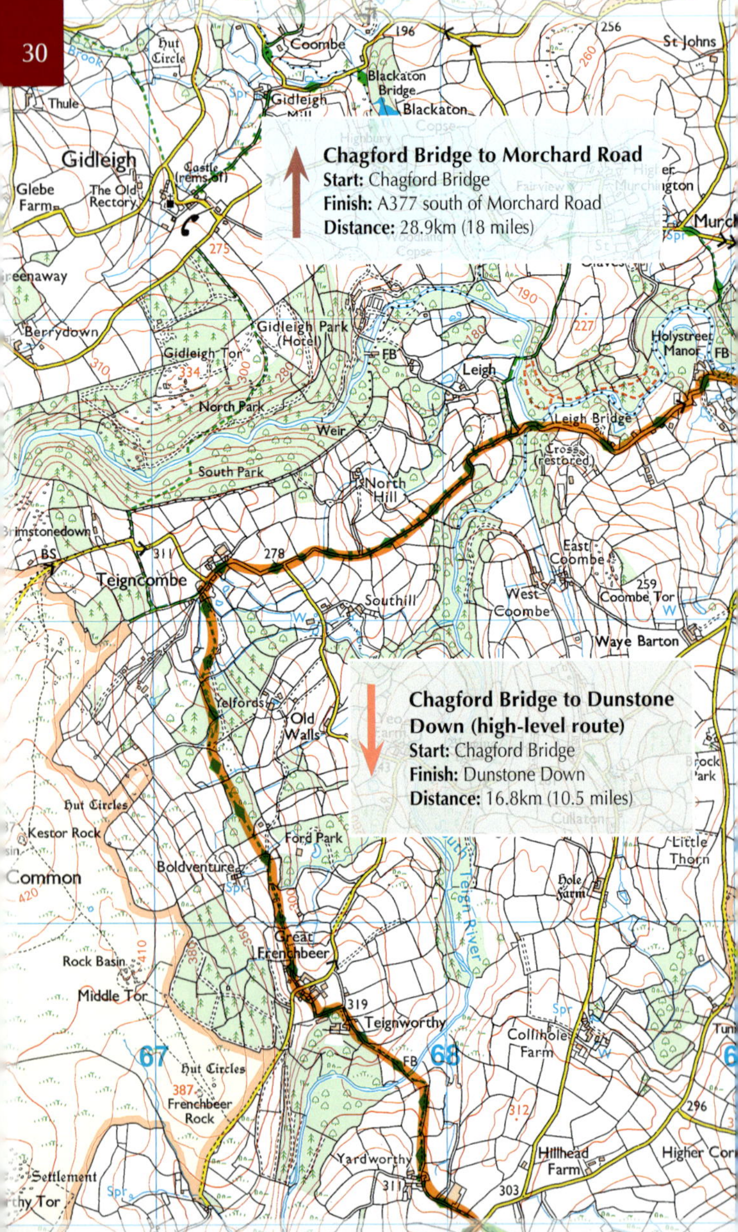

Brook
Hut Circle
Coombe
196
256
St Johns
260
Blackaton Bridge
Gidleigh Mill
Blackaton
Copse
Thule
Gidleigh
Highbury
Fairview
Murchington
Murch
Glebe Farm
Castle (rems of)
The Old Rectory
275
Chagford Bridge to Morchard Road
Start: Chagford Bridge
Finish: A377 south of Morchard Road
Distance: 28.9km (18 miles)
Woodland Copse
Greenaway
190
Gidleigh Park (Hotel)
Graves
Berrydown
Gidleigh Tor
227
Holystreet Manor
FB
310
334
300
280
FB
Leigh
North Park
Weir
Leigh Bridge
South Park
North Hill
Cross (restored)
Brimstonedown
BS
311
278
East Coombe
Teigncombe
Southill
259
Coombe Tor
West Coombe
Waye Barton
Yelfords
Old Walls
Chagford Bridge to Dunstone Down (high-level route)
Start: Chagford Bridge
Finish: Dunstone Down
Distance: 16.8km (10.5 miles)
Brock Park
Hut Circles
Ford Park
Little Thorn
Kestor Rock
Hole Farm
Common
Boldventure
420
South Teign River
Great Frenchbeer
Rock Basin
Middle Tor
410
387
319
Teignworthy
Collihole Farm
67
Hut Circles
68
Frenchbeer Rock
FB
6
312
296
Settlement
Yardworthy
Hillhead Farm
Higher Cor
Tor
311
303

Mount Flaggon
Lower Withecombe
BS
89
Rushford Barton
Weir
Highbury
146
Rushford Mill Farm
Ford
Teign Marsh
B3206
190
180
194
ington
Two Moors Way
Washford Barn
FB
Cuckoofield
Weir
Rushford Br Teign View
157
140
SF
Chagford Bridge
171
88
Teign Link
Dartmoor Way
Hotel
Sch Sch
Chagford
Adley House
Little Weeke
Spr
Kennels
Beechlands
183
Westcott Farm
Great Weeke
Greenacres
P
178
17
Tor Dene
178
Manor Road
P
Chagford House
For
FB
Rec
Dennis Park
Padley Common
W
W
Yellam
29
87
W
Nattadon
Buda Farm
250
200
21
Nattadon Common
333
Week Down Cross
270
233
Meldon Hall
fort
310
324
300
Quintatown
Cross
Meldon Common
350
W
310
390
Meldon Hill
380
Higher Weddicott
Broadalls
Downpark
W
CHAGFORD CP
300
283
86
280
250
288
Lower Weddicott
240
ord
308
Downes
342
70
Higher Stiniel
71
264
230
Lower Corndon
300
Stinhall
Yellands Farm
290
270
Yellands Cross
85
Batw
Beetor Bridge
Western
Jurston

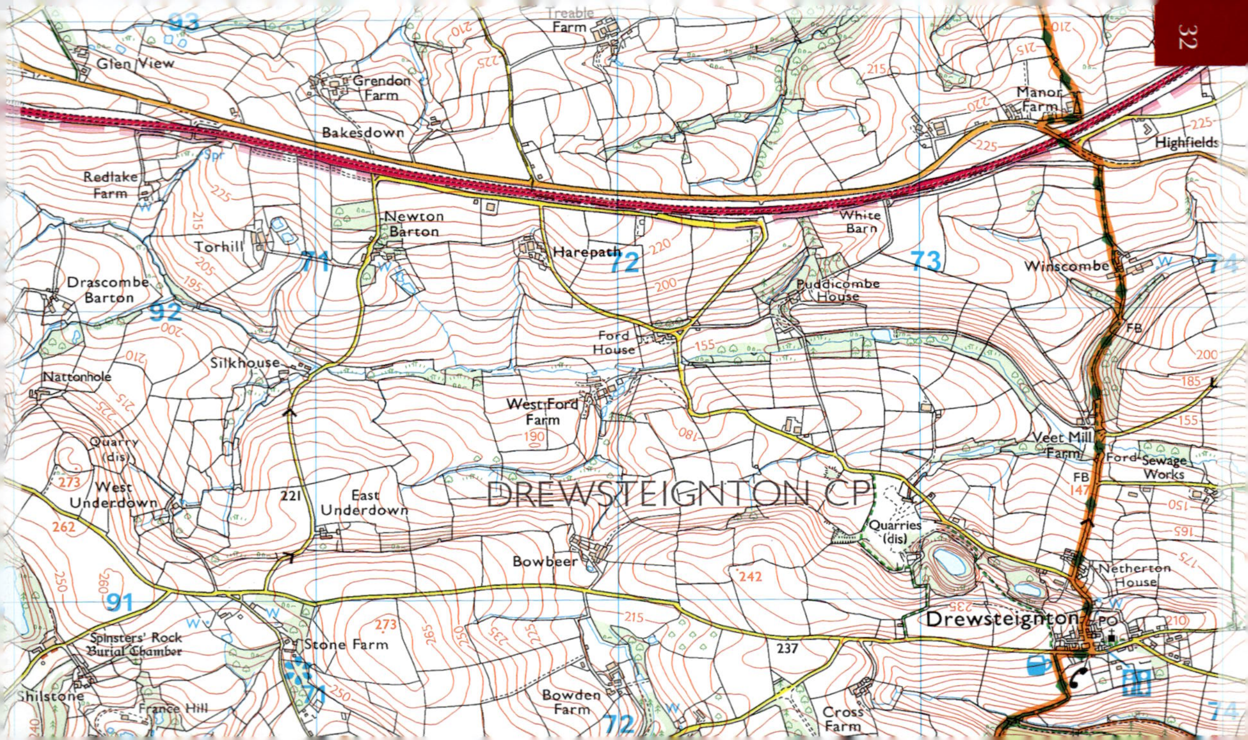
Glen View
Treable Farm
Grendon Farm
Manor Farm
Bakesdown
Highfields
Redlake Farm
White Barn
Winscombe
Newton Barton
Harepath
Puddicombe House
FB
Torhill
Drascombe Barton
Ford House
Silkhouse
Nattonhole
West Ford Farm
Veet Mill Farm
Ford Sewage Works
FB
147
Quarry (dis)
West Underdown
221
East Underdown
DREWSTEIGNTON CP
Quarries (dis)
Bowbeer
242
Netherton House
Spinsters' Rock Burial Chamber
Stone Farm
237
Drewsteignton
PO
Shilstone
France Hill
Bowden Farm
Cross Farm
93
71
72
73
74
92
91
155
190
180
200
215
220
225
273
262
250
260
265
235
185
165
175
150
210
205
195
237

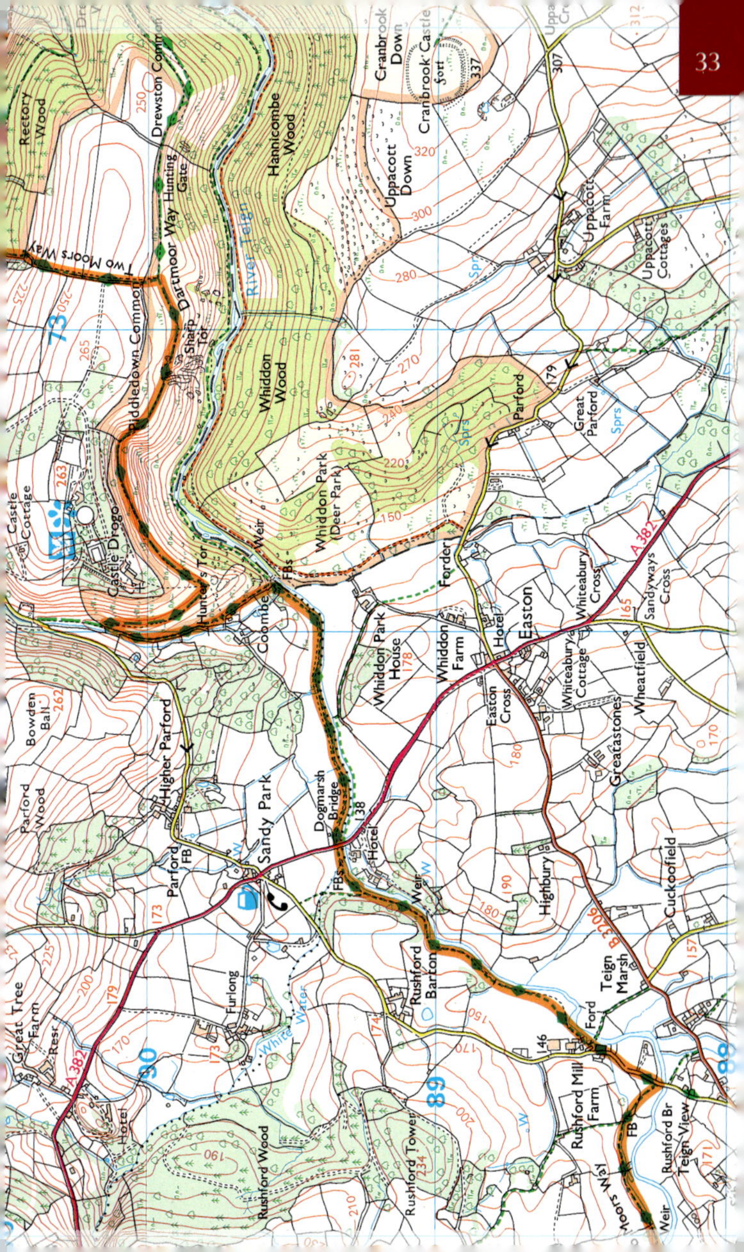

Rectory Wood
Drewston Common
Cranbrook Down
Cranbrook Castle fort
337
312
307
Hunting Gate
Dartmoor Way
Hanniconbe Wood
River Teign
Two Moors Way
250
Uppacott Down
320
300
280
Uppacott Farm
Uppacott Cottages
Piddledown Common
Sharp Tor
265
263
281
270
Whiddon Wood
179
240
Parford
Great Parford
Sprs
220
Whiddon Park (Deer Park)
150
Castle Cottage
Castle Drogo
Weir
FBs
Hunter's Tor
Coombe
Forder
A382
Easton
Whiteabury Cross
Sandyways Cross
165
Whiddon Park House
178
Whiddon Farm
Easton Hotel
Whiteabury Cottage
Whiteabury
Easton Cross
Greatastones
Wheatfield
170
Bowden Ball
262
Higher Parford
Parford Wood
Sandy Park
Dogmarsh Bridge
38
Hotel
180
Highbury
Cuckoofield
Parford FB
W
FBs
Weir
W
190
180
173
Great Tree Farm
Rest.
A382
170
173
Furlong
White Water
174
Rushford Barton
Ford
150
Teign Marsh
157
170
200
146
Rushford Mill Farm
B3206
Rushford Wood
190
Rushford Tower
234
210
Moors Way
Rushford Br Teign View
FB
Weir
171

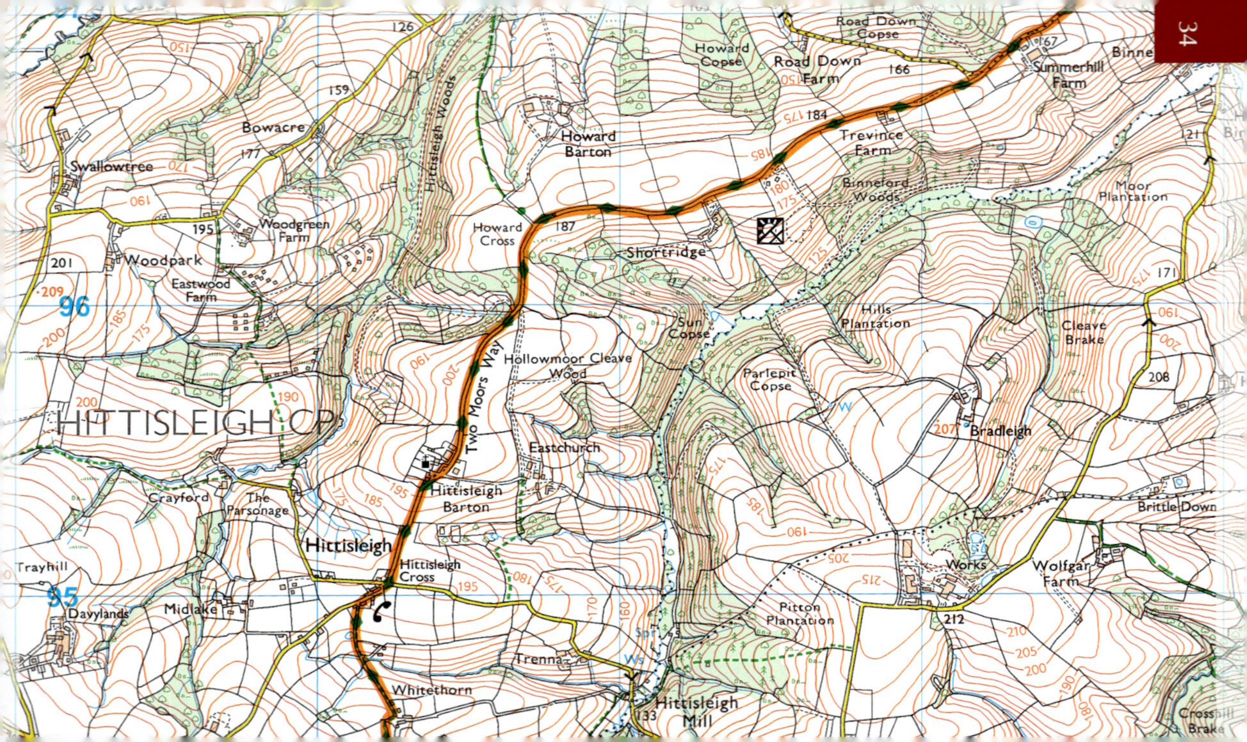
Road Down Copse
Howard Copse
Road Down Farm
Summerhill Farm
Binne
Bowacre
Hittisleigh Woods
Howard Barton
Trevince Farm
Moor Plantation
Swallowtree
Binneford Woods
Woodgreen Farm
Howard Cross
Shortridge
Hills Plantation
Cleave Brake
Woodpark
Sun Copse
Eastwood Farm
Parlepit Copse
Hollowmoor Cleave Wood
HITTISLEIGH CP
Two Moors Way
Eastchurch
Bradleigh
Crayford
The Parsonage
Hittisleigh Barton
Brittle Down
Hittisleigh
Works
Trayhill
Hittisleigh Cross
Wolfgar Farm
Davylands
Midlake
Pitton Plantation
Trenna
Whitethorn
Hittisleigh Mill
Crosshill Brake

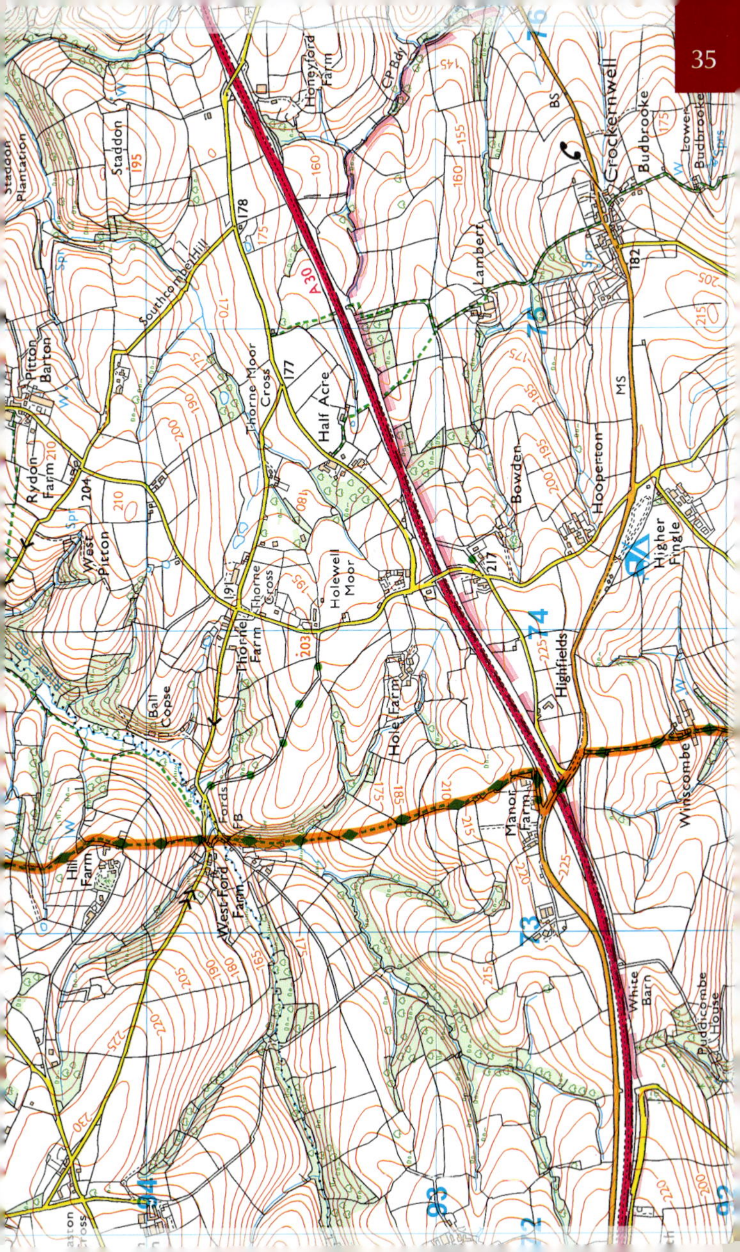

Staddon Plantation
Staddon
195
Southcombe Hill
Honeylord Farm
CP Bdy
145
BS
Crockernwell
Budbrooke
Lower Budbrooke
175
178
175
160
160
155
182
205
A30
Pitton Barton
Rydon Farm
204
210
210
West Pitton
200
190
175
Thorne Moor Cross
177
Half Acre
Holewell Moor
Lambert
175
185
195
Bowden
200
Hooperton
MS
215
215
Higher Fingle
Thorne Cross
191
Thorne Farm
203
195
217
74
Highfields
225
W
Ball Copse
Hole Farm
175
185
210
215
Manor Farm
Winscombe
220
225
Hill Farm
Fords
FB
West-Ford Farm
165
175
180
190
205
215
73
220
225
230
White Barn
Buddicombe House
200
aston Cross
64
63
62
61
76
75

Colebrooke
Colebrooke
Brocks Cross
Brocks
Brocks
Butsford Barton
Horwell Barton
Ford Farm
Broomsland
Six Acre Copse
Seven Acre Brake
COLEBROOKE C P
Tucker's Plot
Horwell Wood
Prestons
Helmoors Down
Whelmstone Barton
Oak Plantation
Two Moors Way
39
47
St Mary's Well
Whelmstone Cross
Landsend Cottages
Landsend Barton
Staddons
Westcombe Hill House
Walson Cross
Walson Barton
Thorne Farm
164
165
160
Middledown Plantation
Higherdown Bottom
Middle Moor
Hilldown Cross
Newcott Farm
77
76
75
74
00
99
157
154
113
133
140
125
105
115
111
100
115
125
135
150
145
130
140

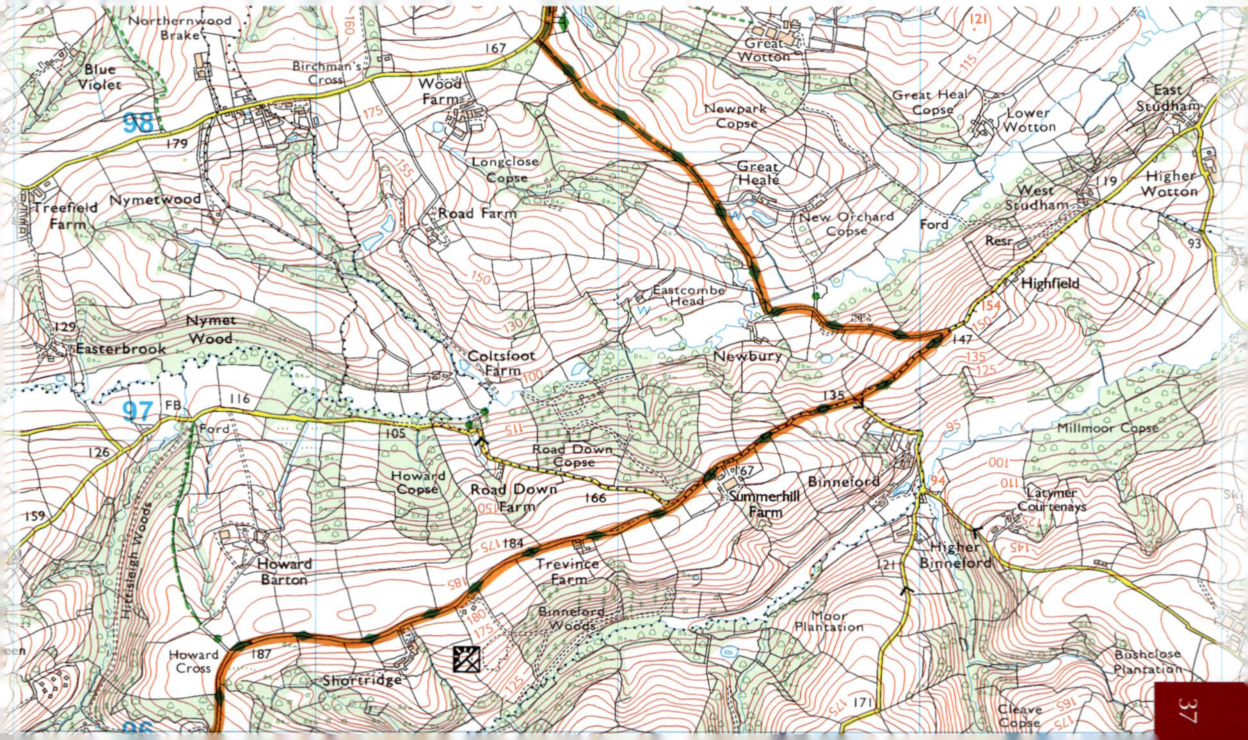

Northernwood Brake
Blue Violet
Birchman's Cross
Wood Farm
Great Wotton
Newpark Copse
Great Heal Copse
Lower Wotton
East Studham
Treefield Farm
Nymetwood
Longclose Copse
Road Farm
Great Heale
New Orchard Copse
Ford
West Studham
Higher Wotton
Resr
Highfield
Easterbrook
Nymet Wood
Eastcombe Head
Coltsfoot Farm
Newbury
Millmoor Copse
FB
Ford
Road Down Copse
Road Down Farm
Howard Copse
Binneford
Latymer Courtenays
Summerhill Farm
Higher Binneford
Hittisleigh Woods
Howard Barton
Trevince Farm
Binneford Woods
Moor Plantation
Howard Cross
Shortridge
Bushclose Plantation
Cleave Copse
167
160
175
179
98
155
150
130
154
150
135
125
100
135
95
94
100
110
129
116
97
105
115
126
159
166
150
67
175
184
185
121
145
180
175
125
171
175
187
96

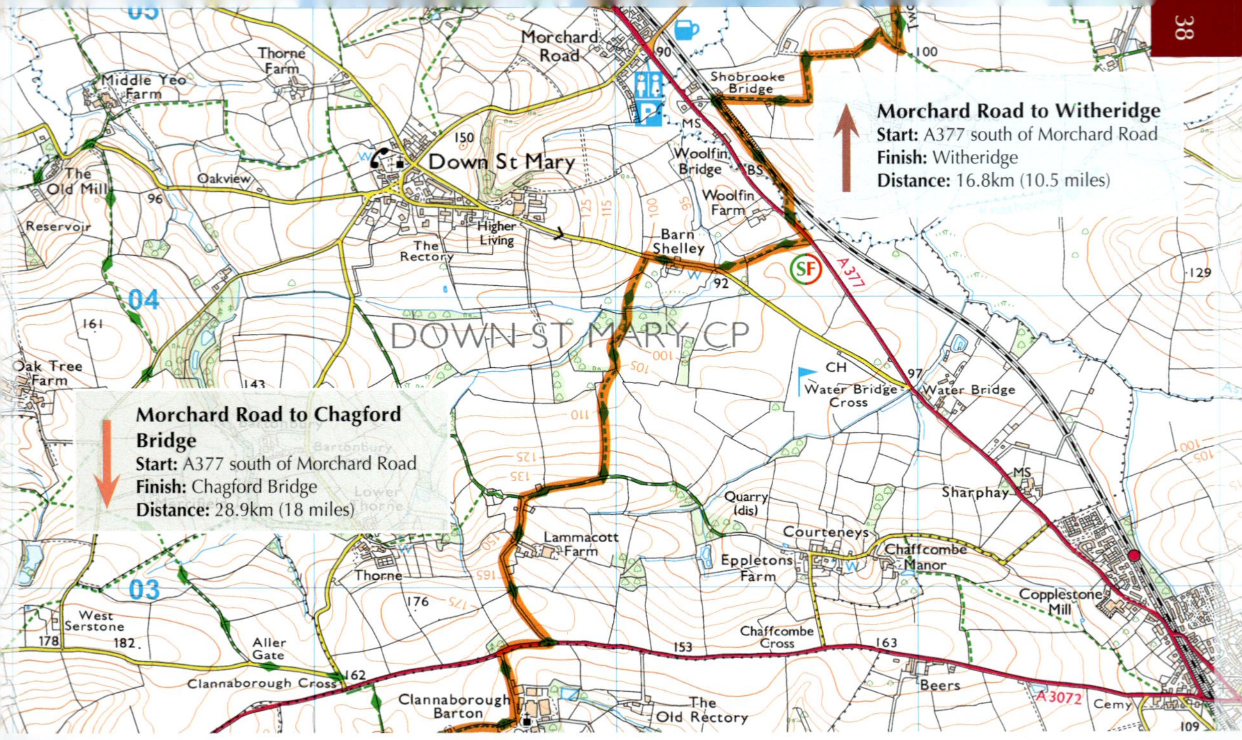

Morchard Road to Witheridge
Start: A377 south of Morchard Road
Finish: Witheridge
Distance: 16.8km (10.5 miles)

Morchard Road to Chagford Bridge
Start: A377 south of Morchard Road
Finish: Chagford Bridge
Distance: 28.9km (18 miles)

DOWN ST MARY CP
Down St Mary
Morchard Road
Thorne Farm
Middle Yeo Farm
The Old Mill
Oakview
Reservoir
Oak Tree Farm
Higher Living
The Rectory
Shobrooke Bridge
Woolfin Bridge
Woolfin Farm
Barn Shelley
Water Bridge Cross
Water Bridge
CH
Sharphay
Quarry (dis)
Courteneys
Eppletons Farm
Chaffcombe Manor
Lammacott Farm
Chaffcombe Cross
Copplestone Mill
Thorne
West Serstone
Aller Gate
Clannaborough Cross
Clannaborough Barton
The Old Rectory
Beers
A377
A3072
MS
BS
SF

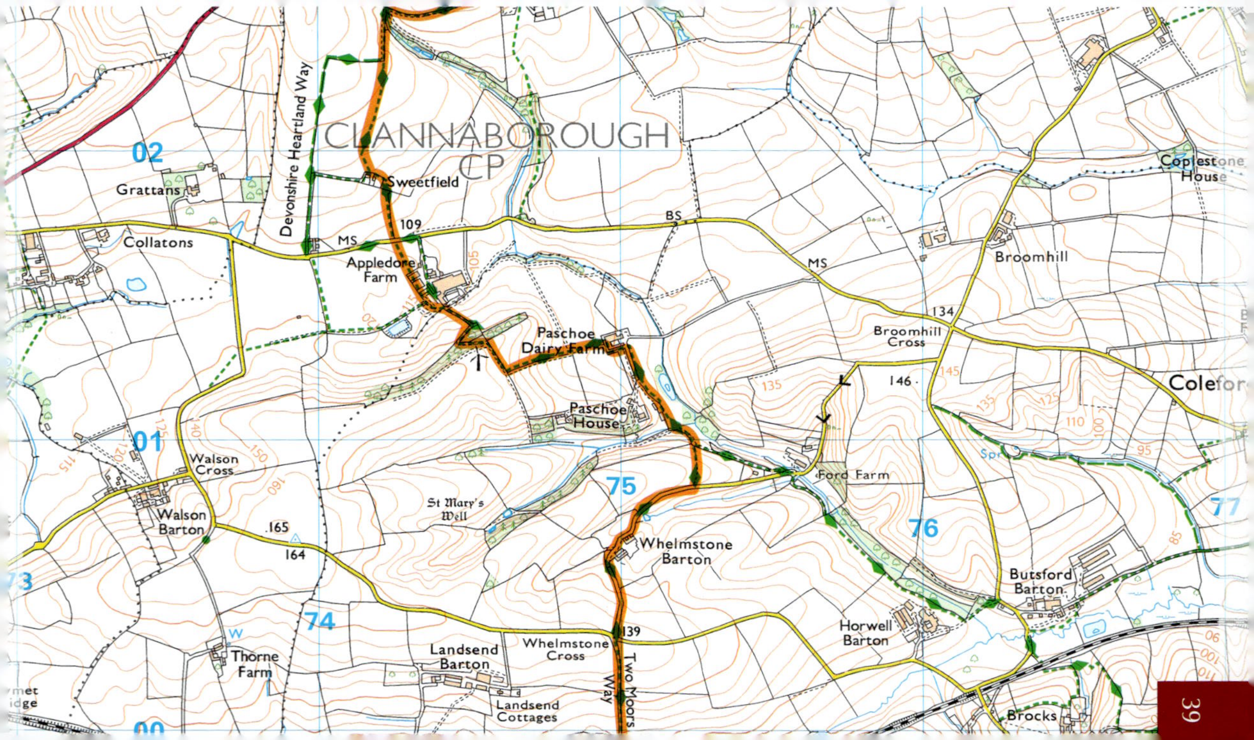
CLANNABOROUGH CP
Devonshire Heartland Way
Sweetfield
Grattans
Collatons
Appledore Farm
109
MS
BS
Copplestone House
Broomhill
Paschoe Dairy Farm
Broomhill Cross
134
146
145
Coleford
105
MS
Paschoe House
135
Ford Farm
Walson Cross
St Mary's Well
75
76
77
Walson Barton
165
164
Whelmstone Barton
Butsford Barton
73
74
Horwell Barton
Thorne Farm
Whelmstone Cross
Landsend Barton
139
Two Moors Way
Landsend Cottages
Brocks
00
met idge
39

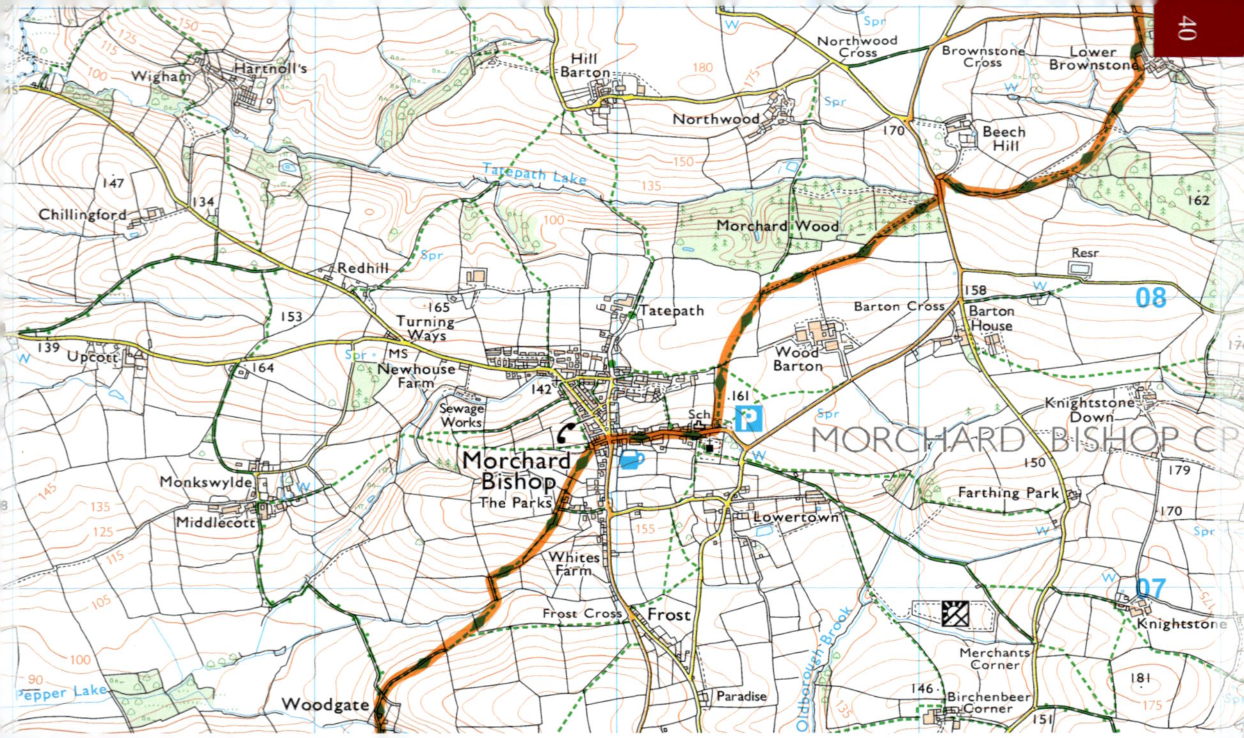
Wigham
Hartnoll's
Hill Barton
Northwood Cross
Brownstone Cross
Lower Brownstone
180
175
170
Northwood
Beech Hill
147
134
Tatepath Lake
150
135
162
Chillingford
100
Morchard Wood
Resr
Redhill
158
153
165
Tatepath
Barton Cross
Barton House
08
Turning Ways
139
Upcott
MS
Newhouse Farm
164
Wood Barton
161
142
Sch
Knightstone Down
MORCHARD BISHOP CP
Sewage Works
Morchard Bishop
The Parks
150
179
Monkswylde
155
Lowertown
Farthing Park
170
Middlecott
145
135
125
115
Whites Farm
07
105
Frost Cross
Frost
Knightstone
175
100
Oldborough Brook
Merchants Corner
90
Pepper Lake
Woodgate
Paradise
135
146
Birchenbeer Corner
181
151

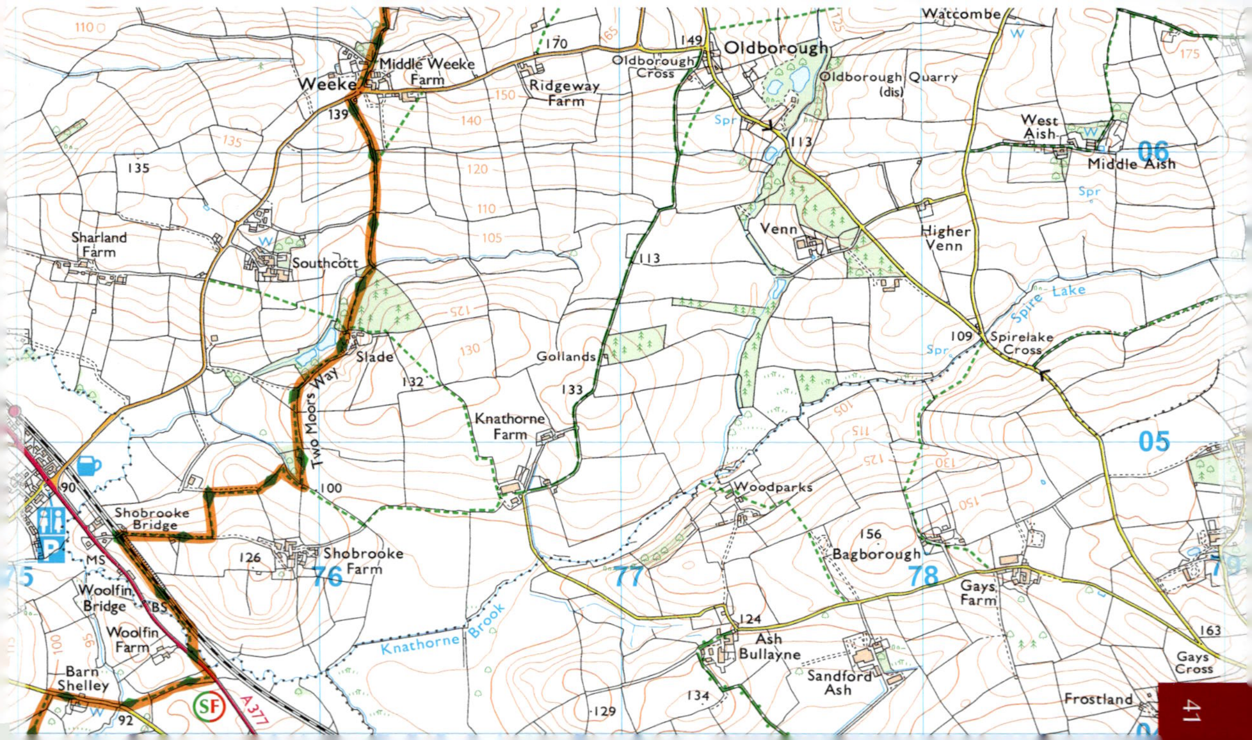

Watcombe
110
170
165
149
Oldborough
125
W
Oldborough Cross
Oldborough Quarry (dis)
175
Middle Weeke Farm
Weeke
Ridgeway Farm
Spr
West Aish
W
139
150
140
113
06
135
135
120
Middle Aish
Spr
110
105
Venn
Higher Venn
Sharland Farm
W
Southcott
113
Spire Lake
109
Spirelake Cross
Spr
125
130
Gollands
133
05
Slade
132
Knathorne Farm
115
125
105
Two Moors Way
Woodparks
130
150
100
156
Bagborough
90
Shobrooke Bridge
126
Shobrooke Farm
76
77
78
MS
75
Woolfin Bridge
BS
124
Ash Bullayne
Gays Farm
Woolfin Farm
Knathorne Brook
163
Barn Shelley
SF
A 377
92
W
129
134
Sandford Ash
Gays Cross
Frostland
41

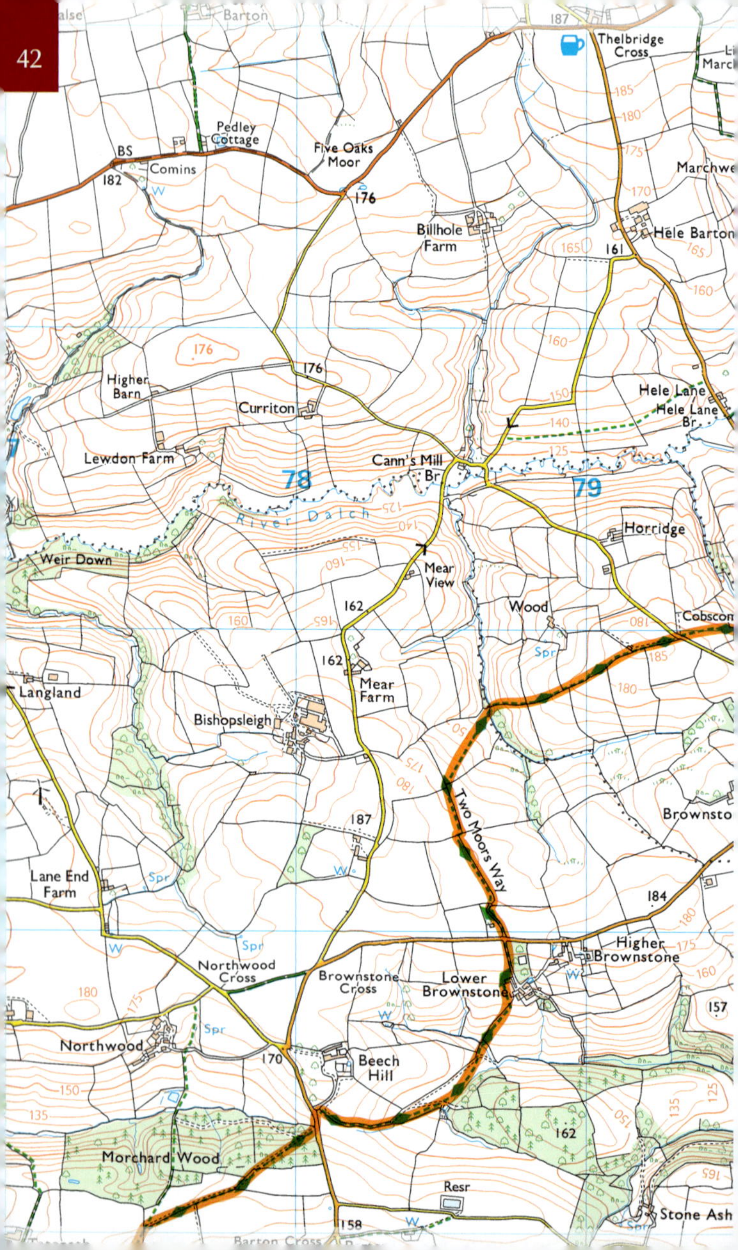
Barton
187
Thelbridge Cross
Li
Marc
185
180
Pedley Cottage
175
Five Oaks Moor
Marchwe
170
BS
Comins
182
176
Billhole Farm
165
161
Hele Barton
160
165
176
Higher Barn
150
Hele Lane
Hele Lane Br
176
Curriton
140
Lewdon Farm
Cann's Mill Br
125
78
79
River Dalch
125
Horridge
140
Weir Down
155
160
Mear View
162
Wood
Cobscon
160
165
081
Spr
185
162
Langland
Mear Farm
180
Bishopsleigh
175
180
Two Moors Way
187
Brownsto
184
Lane End Farm
Spr
Higher Brownstone
175
Spr
Northwood Cross
Brownstone Cross
Lower Brownstone
160
180
157
Northwood
170
Beech Hill
150
135
162
Morchard Wood
Resr
135
125
Stone Ash
158
Barton Cross

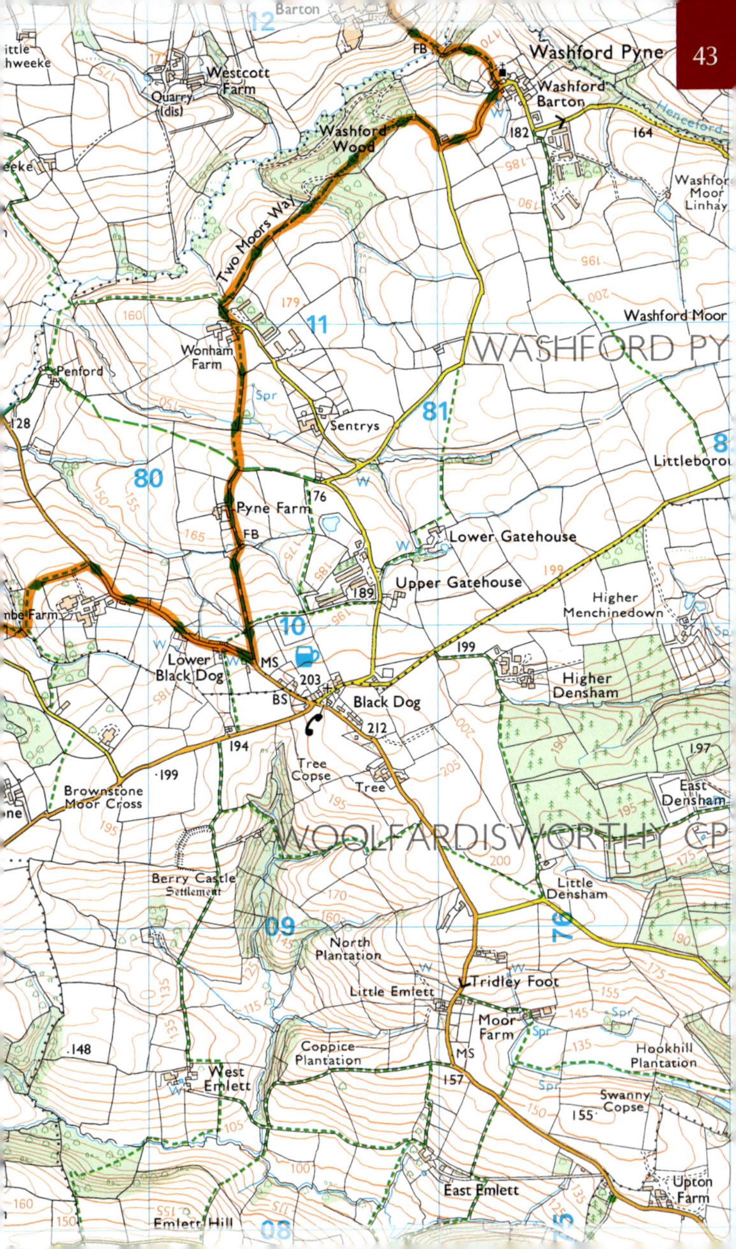

43
Barton
Washford Pyne
FB
Washford Barton
Westcott Farm
Little hweeke
Quarry (dis)
Washford Wood
Henceford
182
164
Washford Moor Linhay
eeke
Two Moors Way
175
160
179
11
Washford Moor
WASHFORD PY
Wonham Farm
Penford
Spr
128
80
Sentrys
81
8
Littleborou
150
155
165
Pyne Farm
76
FB
Lower Gatehouse
W
Upper Gatehouse
199
Higher Menchinedown
189
nbe Farm
10
195
199
Lower Black Dog
W
MS
203
Black Dog
199
Higher Densham
BS
212
197
194
Tree Copse
205
East Densham
199
Brownstone Moor Cross
Tree
195
WOOLFARDISWORTHY CP
200
Berry Castle Settlement
09
Little Densham
78
North Plantation
190
148
Little Emlett
Tridley Foot
175
West Emlett
Coppice Plantation
Moor Farm
MS
Spr
Hookhill Plantation
157
150
155
Swanny Copse
160
150
155
105
100
Emlett Hill
08
East Emlett
Upton Farm

Witheridge to Knowstone

Start: Witheridge
Finish: Knowstone
Distance: 12.5km (7.8 miles)

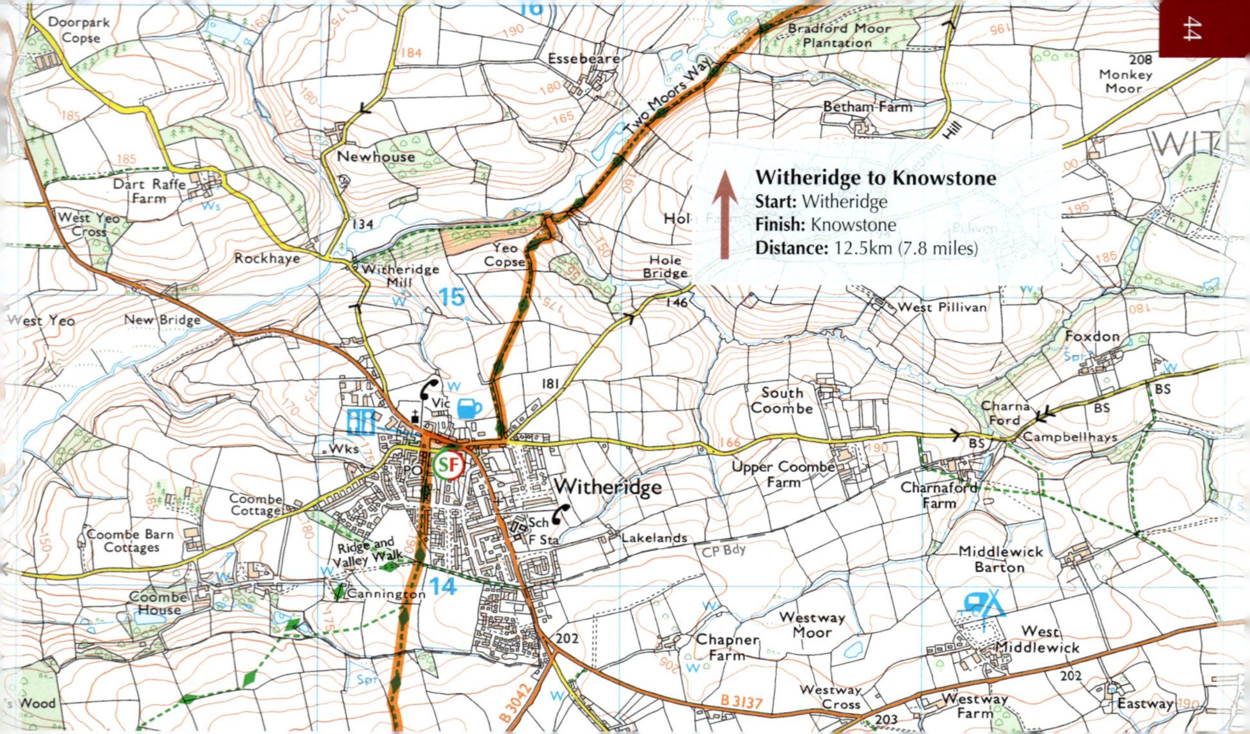

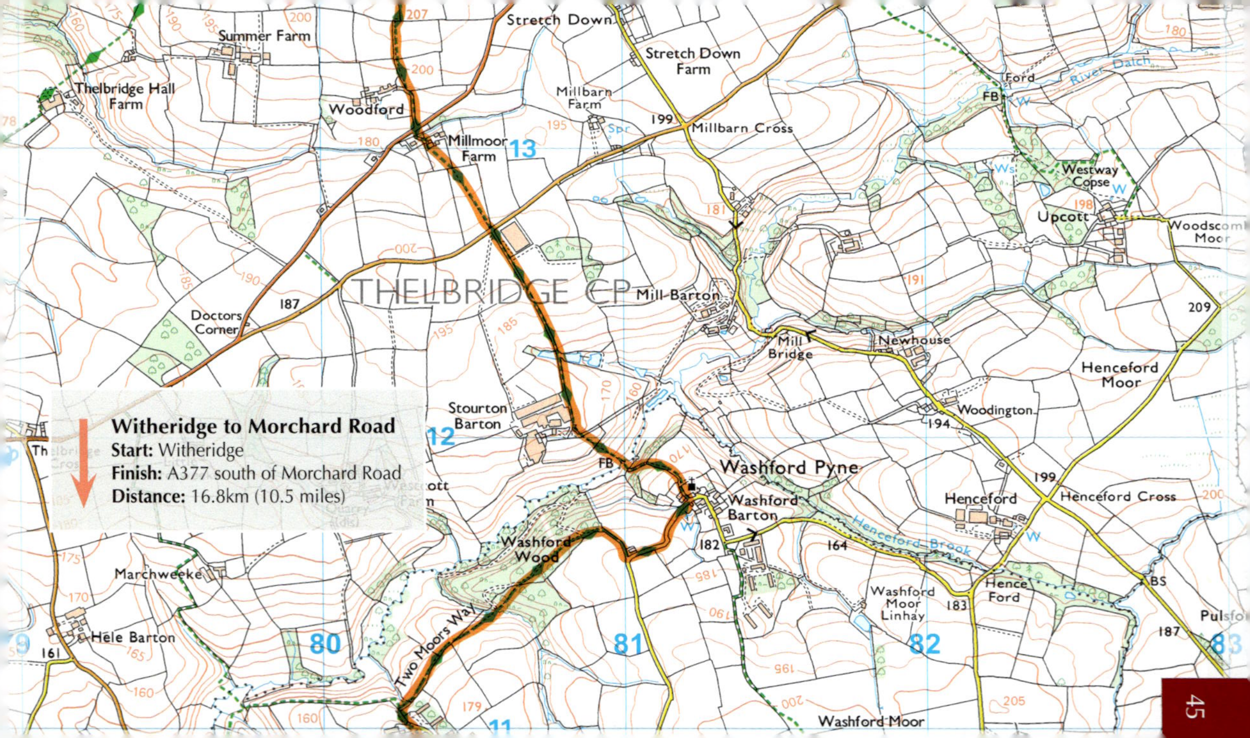
Stretch Down
Stretch Down Farm
Ford
FB
River Dart
Summer Farm
Thelbridge Hall Farm
Woodford
Millbarn Farm
199
Millbarn Cross
Westway Copse
Millmoor Farm
13
Upcott
198
Woodscombe Moor
THELBRIDGE CP
Mill Barton
191
209
Doctors Corner
187
Mill Bridge
Newhouse
Henceford Moor
Stourton Barton
12
Woodington
194
Washford Pyne
199
Henceford
Henceford Cross
200
FB
Washford Barton
Henceford Brook
W
Washford Wood
182
164
Marchweeke
Washford Moor Linhay
Hence Ford
183
BS
Two Moors Way
Hele Barton
187
Pulsfo
161
80
81
82
83
11
Washford Moor
205

Witheridge to Morchard Road
Start: Witheridge
Finish: A377 south of Morchard Road
Distance: 16.8km (10.5 miles)

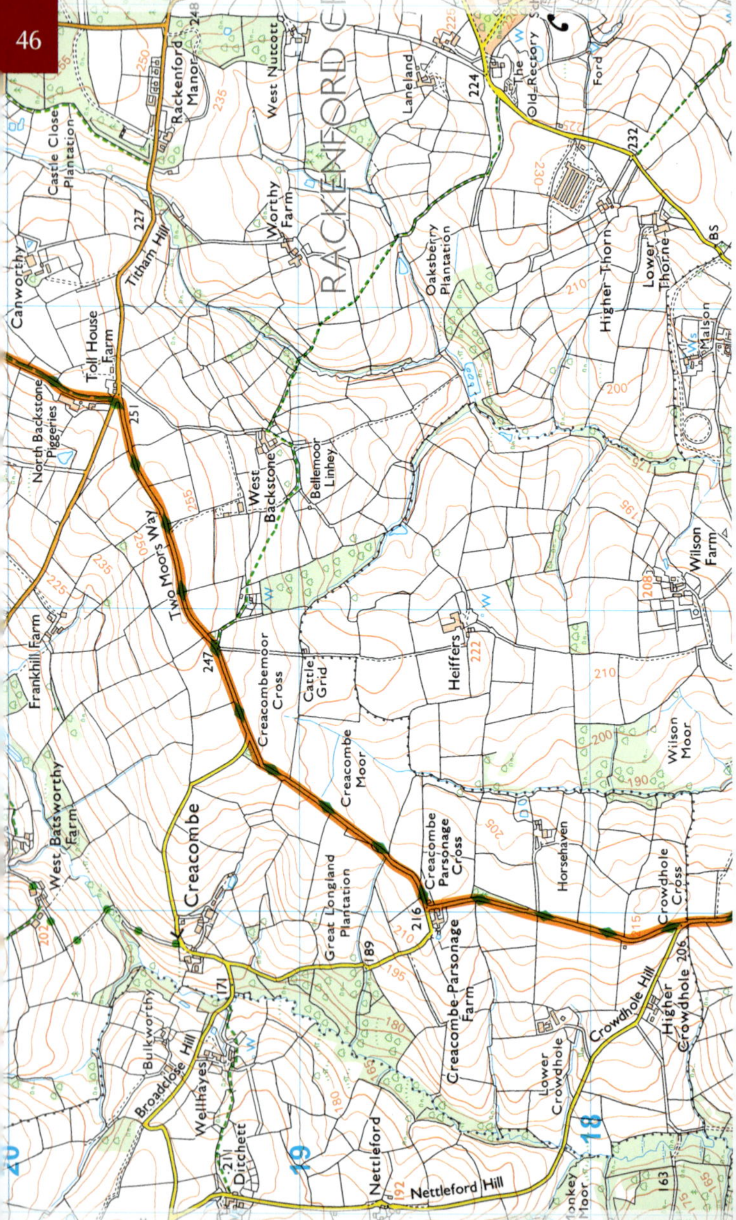
Rackenford Manor
248
West Nuttcott
RACKENFORD CP
Laneland
224
The Old Rectory
Ford
Castle Close Plantation
250
235
227
Worthy Farm
Oaksberry Plantation
225
232
Higher Thorn
Lower Thorne
BS
Canworthy
Titham Hill
230
210
200
Ws
Malson
Toll House Farm
251
West Backstone
Bellemoor Linhey
Two Moors Way
255
W
Wilson Farm
North Backstone Piggeries
250
235
225
195
208
210
Frankhill Farm
247
Creacombemoor Cross
Cattle Grid
Heiffers
222
200
Wilson Moor
190
Creacombe Moor
205
Creacombe Parsonage Cross
Horsehaven
200
West Batsworthy Farm
Creacombe
Great Longland Plantation
216
216
Crowdhole Cross
215
202
189
210
195
Creacombe-Parsonage Farm
Crowdhole Hill
206
Bulkworthy
Broadclose Hill
Wellhayes
W
171
180
165
Lower Crowdhole
Higher Crowdhole
163
165
Ditchett
19
Nettleford
Monkey Moor
18
20
192
Nettleford Hill

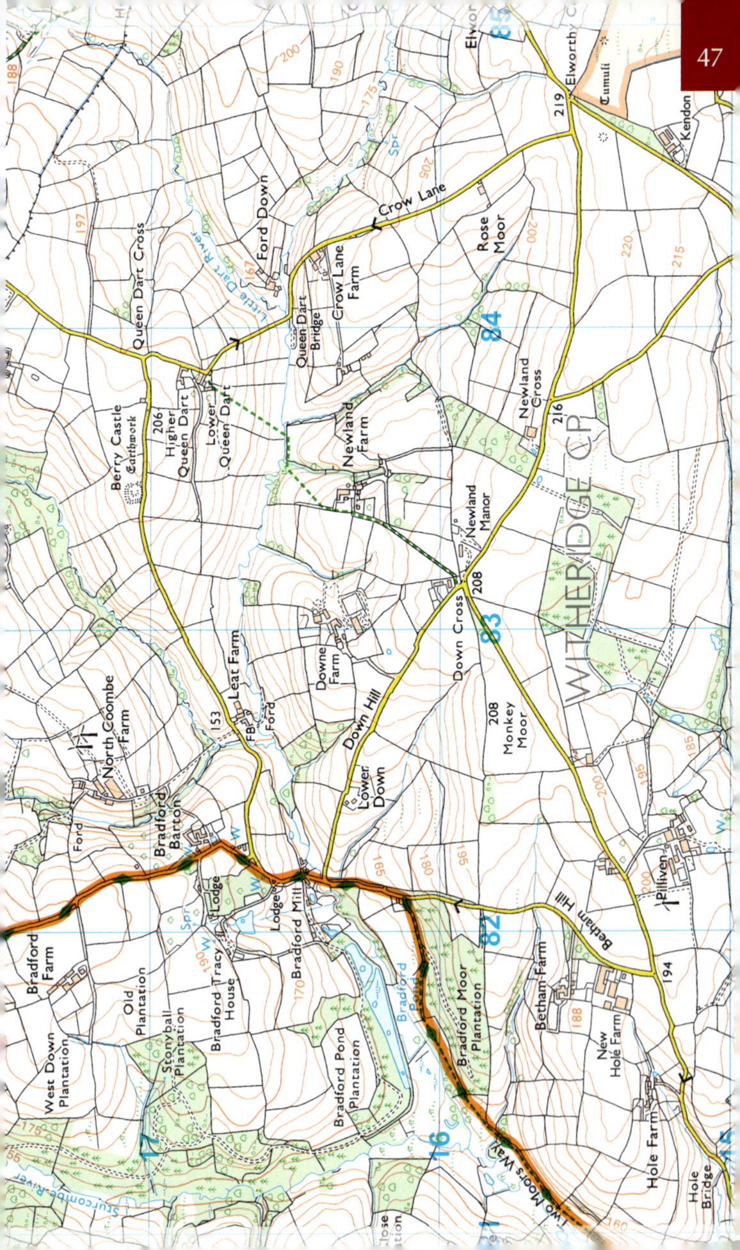
188
200
190
175
197
Little Dart River
Queen Dart Cross
Ford Down
Crow Lane
Spr
205
207
Rose Moor
Elworth
219
Tumuli
Kendon
85
84
200
220
215
Berry Castle Earthwork
206
Higher Queen Dart
Lower Queen Dart
Queen Dart Bridge
Crow Lane Farm
Newland Farm
Newland Cross
216
WITHERIDGE CP
North Coombe Farm
Bradford Barton
Ford
153
Leat Farm
FB
Ford
Downe Farm
Down Hill
Newland Manor
Down Cross
208
83
208
Monkey Moor
195
185
Lower Down
Pilliven
200
West Down Plantation
Old Plantation
Stonyball Plantation
Bradford Tracy House
Lodge
Lodge
Bradford Mill
170
Bradford Pond Plantation
Bradford Pond
Bradford Moor Plantation
82
Betham Farm
Betham Hill
188
194
Bradford Farm
190
Spr
165
180
165
New Hole Farm
Hole Farm
17
16
175
155
Sturcombe River
Two Moors Way
160
Hole Bridge

Knowstone to Tarr Steps
Start: Knowstone
Finish: Tarr Steps
Distance: 17.5km (11 miles)

Poole Wood
Farm
Three Acre Plantation
Poole Moor
254
Batsworthy Cross Wind Farm
Batsworthy Cross
Castle Moor
Lower Moor
82
219
Moortown Barton
Manor Farm
Great Comfort Farm
Little Oak
A361
Spr
21
Knowstone Outer Moor
269
Hares D
244
Ford
Moortown Moor
83
North Plantation
Hares Down Cross
In Moor
84
Canworthy Common
Waterloo Farm
North Backstone
Canworthy
Worthy Moor House
258
Castle Close Plantation
24
Knowstone to Witheridge
Start: Knowstone
Finish: Witheridge
Distance: 12.5km (7.8 miles)
Frankhill Farm
North Backstone Piggeries
Toll House Farm
251
227
Titham Hill
Two Moors Way
Rackenford Manor
248
Worthy Farm
West
Broadclose Hill
Bulkworthy
Wellhayes
171
Ditchett
211
Creacombe
247
Creacombemoor Cross
West Backstone
Cattle
49

Whitley Wood
Netherwell Farm
Guphill Wood
Woodland Farm
Badlake Lane
Churchtown Farm
258
244
Badlake Farm
West Anstey
Town Farm
241
245
Two Moors Way
240
Beere Wood
232
Deer's Leap Farm
Wood's Copse
250
Beech
East Lee Wood
Slade Wood
Town Farm Wood
Town Hill
Woods
Hill Farm
W
Ash
Oak
Beer Farm
Bidbrook
Beechdale
Slade
167
Wood's Cross
206
226
East Lee
Spr
210
Dunsley Mill
New Park Farm
183
Spr
Ruggleplitt
Valaford
River Yeo
153
Lower Wychwood
Dunsley
194
Sheep Dip
148
Mill House
Bottreaux Mill
West Park
Partridge Arms Farm
Yeo Mill
Hall
Bunksland Farm
165
Three Gables
EAST ANSTEY
190
Barton Wood
West Barton
175
Lands Farm
Two Moors Way
Lower Radnidge Farm
Dunsley Moors
Bommertown Cross
Cuckoo Farm
East Barton
Sing Moor
177
200
Higher R
Great Copse

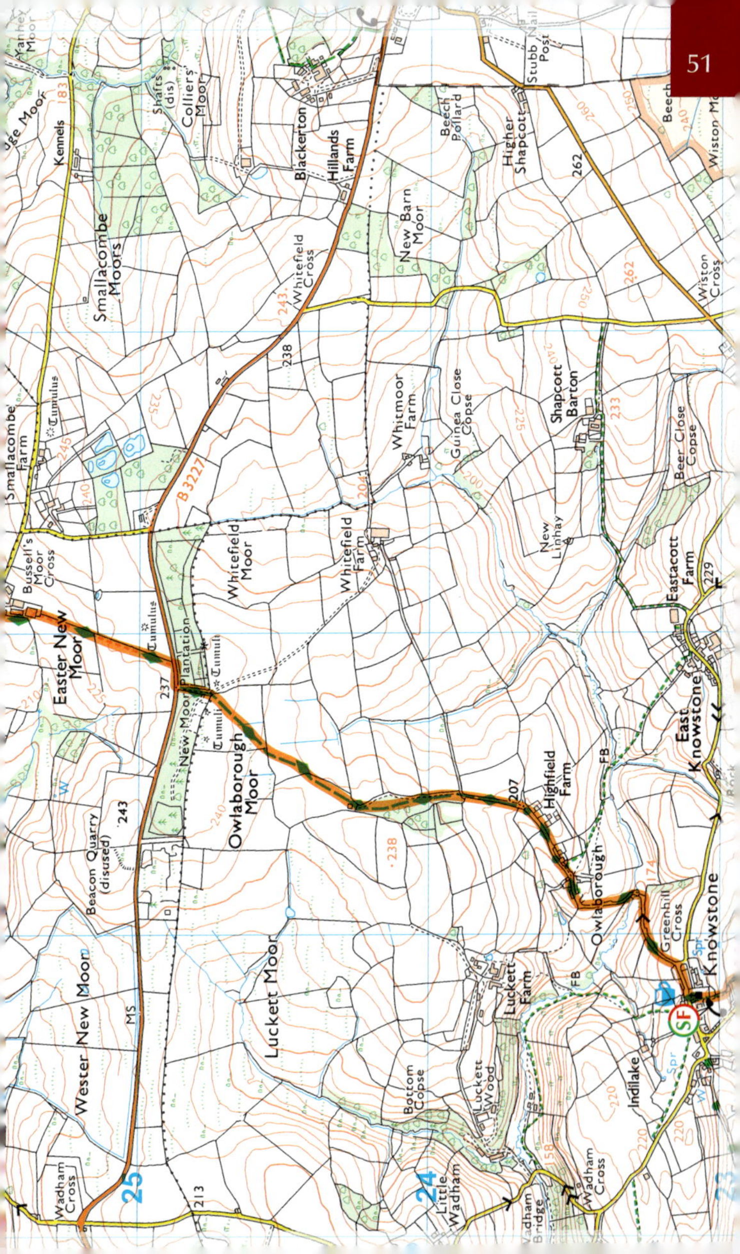
Yathey Moor
Oge Moor
Kennels
Shafts (dis)
Colliers' Moor
Blackerton
Hillands Farm
New Barn Moor
Beech Pollard
Higher Shapcott
Stubb Post
Beech
Wiston Moor
Wiston Cross
Smallacombe Moors
183
245
Tumulus
235
240
Smallacombe Farm
238
Whitefield Cross
243
Whitmoor Farm
Guinea Close Copse
225
New Linhay
Shapcott Barton
233
Beer Close Copse
262
262
250
200
204
B 3227
Bussell's Moor Cross
Whitefield Moor
Whitefield Farm
Easter New Moor
Tumulus
237
New Moor Plantation
Tumuli
Tumulus
Tumulus
Eastacott Farm
229
East Knowstone
210
225
240
Owlaborough Moor
Highfield Farm
207
FB
Beacon Quarry (disused)
243
174
Owlaborough
Greenhill Cross
Spr
Wester New Moor
Luckett Moor
238
Luckett Farm
FB
Knowstone
SF
MS
Bottom Copse
Luckett Wood
Indilake
220
158
220
220
Wadham Cross
213
25
Little Wadham
24
Wadham Bridge
Wadham Cross

32
31
30
88
87
86
85
26
Parsonage Farm
South Barton Wood
Ashway Side
Ashway Hat Wood
Row Down Wood
Penny Bridge
Withypool Cross
338
Hawkridge Common
Quarries (disused)
Quarry (dis)
Ashway
Sheepfolds
Tarr Post
358
Workings (dis)
352
Great Cleeve
Cinder Pool
CG
Wester Shircombe
Marshclose Hill
H Ram
Shircombe Farm
Hawkridge Cross
Two Waters
Nine Acre Copse
Slade
FB
296
East Hollowcombe
Hawkridge
Little Birchcleeve Wood
Row Lane
295
Three Waters
Lyshwell Wood
287
Slade Lane
West Hollowcombe
Exe Valley Way
Horse Wood
Shircombe Brake
Zeal Brake
West Hollowcombe Wood
Great Birchcleeve Wood
Hawkridge Ridge
Great Gate
259
Zeal Farm
Great Common
Ford
Dane's Brook
Anstey Rhiney Moor
Venford Ford Wood
Ford
West Anstey Common
Yamson Coppice
Ford
308
Buckminster Wood

Common
Long Stone
Hamson Linhay
Winterocks Down
309
Guphill Common
West Anstey Barrows
333
350
356
Ridge Road
Two Moors Way
Venford
25
29
311
Venford Moor
300
325
Woodland Plantation
296
240
351
BS
East Anstey Common
Ansty Barrow
Liscombe Allotment
Five Cross Ways
297
Cattle Grid
Woodland Common
325
Twitchen Common
3
WEST ANSTEY CP
Spr
Badlake Moor Cross
West Anstey Farm
Rhyll Gate Cross
315
295
Rockswood Plantation
Cattle Grid
300
Rhyll Gate
Guphill
Blindwell
255
290
275
24
Badlake Lane
Spr
28
Chiltons Farm
Higntertown
East Liscombe
250
231
Guphill Wood
250
Woodland Farm
245
275
Churchtown Farm
244
258
West Liscombe
238
Spr
241
Spr
Badlake Farm
Rhyll Manor
267
Wood's Copse
250
West Anstey
Town Hill Woods
oors Way
240
Beech
Waddicombe
Henspark
Combe Lane
Liscombe Wood
Sprs
Oldway Road
Spr
Woods
Spr
Ash
Ford
FB
Oak
Armer Wood
27
53

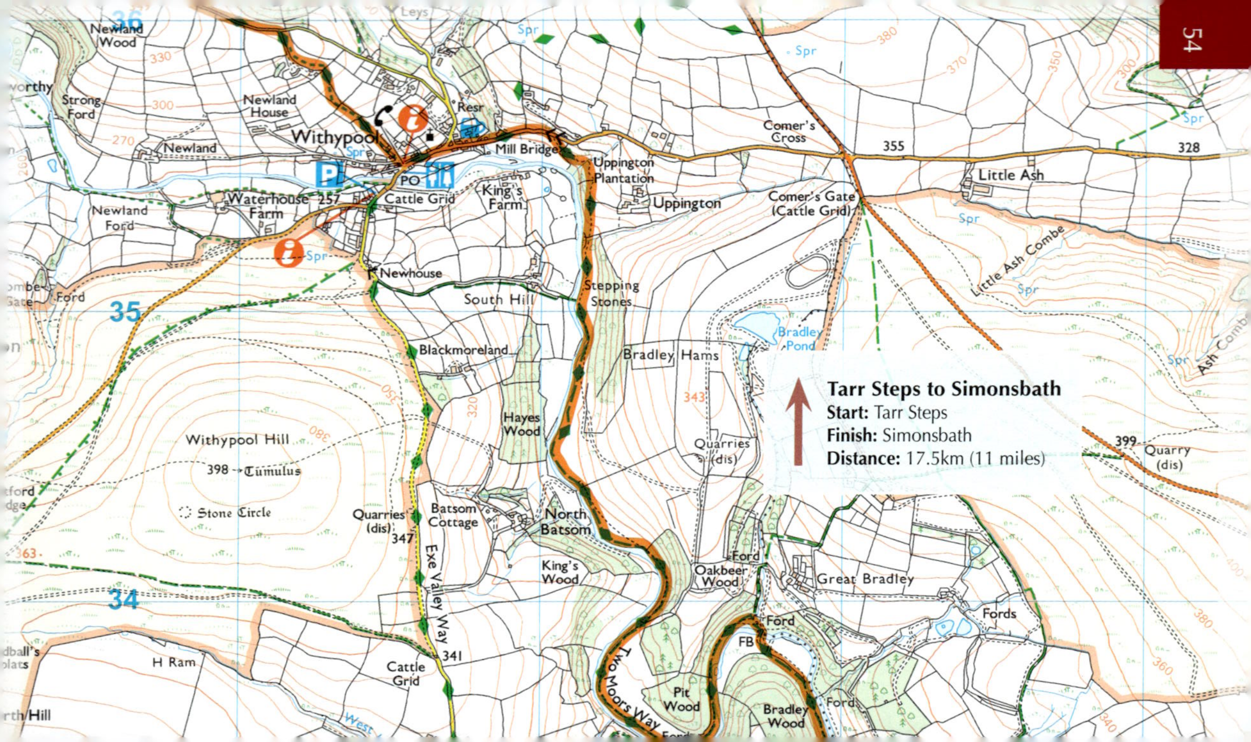
Tarr Steps to Simonsbath
Start: Tarr Steps
Finish: Simonsbath
Distance: 17.5km (11 miles)
Newland Wood
Strong Ford
Newland House
Newland
Withypool
Resr
Mill Bridge
Comer's Cross
355
328
Little Ash
Comer's Gate (Cattle Grid)
Uppington Plantation
Uppington
Little Ash Combe
Newland Ford
Waterhouse Farm
257
Cattle Grid
King's Farm
PO
Newhouse
South Hill
Stepping Stones
Bradley Pond
Ash Combe
Blackmoreland
Bradley Hams
343
Quarries (dis)
399
Quarry (dis)
Withypool Hill
398
Tumulus
Hayes Wood
Stone Circle
Quarries (dis)
347
Batsom Cottage
North Batsom
King's Wood
Exe Valley Way
Oakbeer Wood
Ford
Great Bradley
Fords
H Ram
Cattle Grid
341
Two Moors Way
Pit Wood
FB
Ford
Bradley Wood
Ford
36
35
34
330
300
270
260
380
370
350
320
350
380
360
340
363
Spr
West

Ford
Worth
H Ram
Lea Wood
Knaplock
Higher Knaplock
Westwater Farm
305
Worth Wood
280
294
300
320
Westwater Allotment
33
Westwater Linhay
316
FB
Watery Lane
Quarry (dis)
Old Barrow Plantation
340
300
Parsonage Down
Westwater Copse
Ford
Knaplock Wood
390
Old Barrow Down
388
84
Old Barrow
373
85
North Barton Wood
86
Tarr Steps Woodland
National Nature Reserve
87
325
Tarr Steps (FB)
Tarr Farm
Fords
SF
Spr
Ashwa
32
359
Hill Farm
Parsonage Farm
South Barton Wood
Sprs
Clogg's Down
Tarr Steps to Knowstone
Start: Tarr Steps
Finish: Knowstone
Distance: 17.5km (11 miles)
Row Down Wood
Penny Bridge
kridge Common
Ashway Hat Wood
Cinder Pool
290
310
270
230
200
Quarry (dis)
Ashway
Cloggs Farm
Workings (dis)
352
Great Cleeve
Close Hill
Spr
31
Wester Shircombe
Hawkridge
55

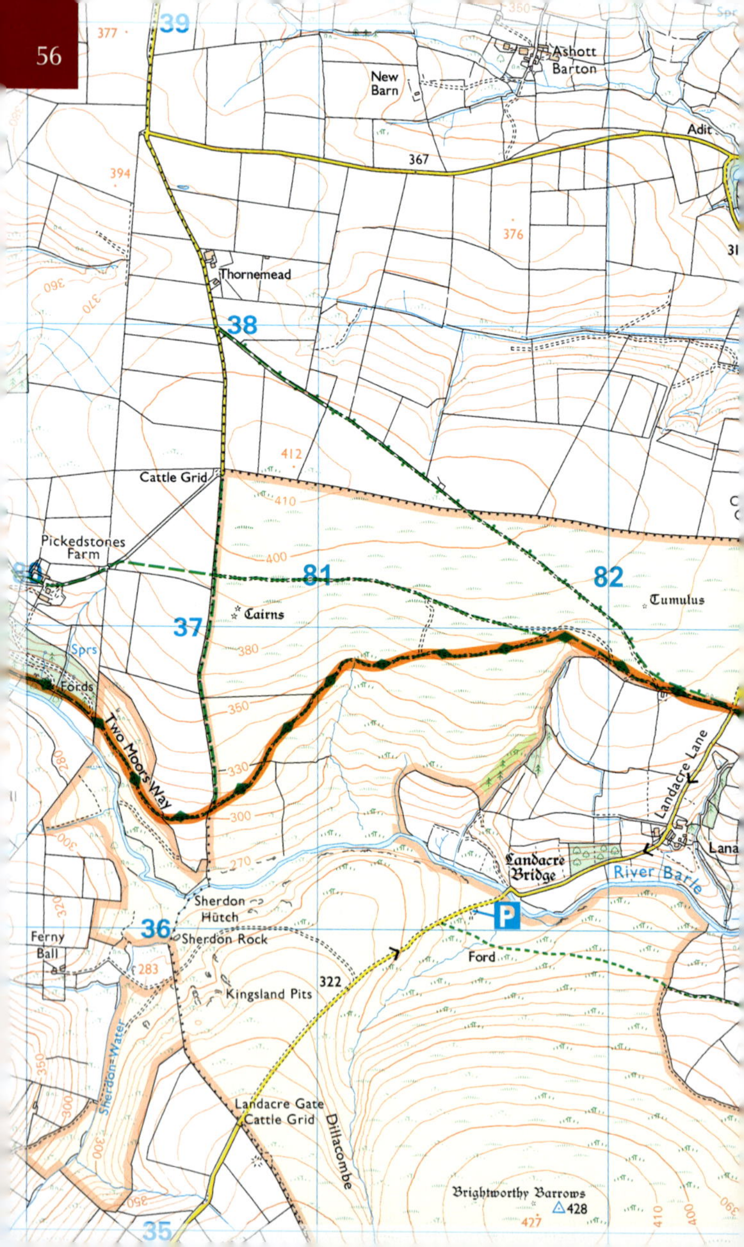

56
377
39
350
Ashott Barton
New Barn
Adit
367
394
376
31
360
370
Thornemead
38
412
Cattle Grid
410
Pickedstones Farm
400
81
82
86
Tumulus
Cairns
37
380
Sprs
Fords
350
Two Moors Way
330
Landacre Lane
280
300
270
Landacre Bridge
River Barle
Lana
320
Sherdon Hutch
P
Ferny Ball
36
Sherdon Rock
Ford
283
322
Kingsland Pits
Sherdon Water
300
350
Landacre Gate
Cattle Grid
Dillacombe
300
350
Brightworthy Barrows
428
427
410
400
35

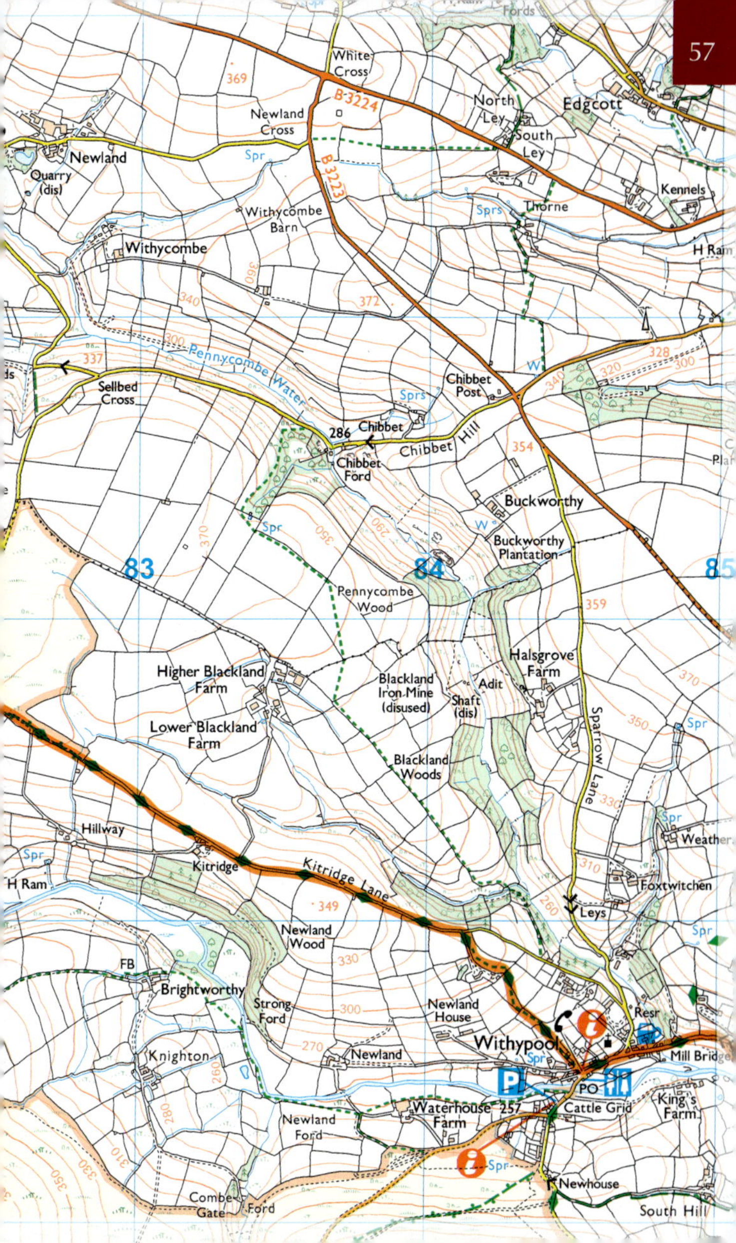
White Cross
B 3224
Newland Cross
369
Newland
Quarry (dis)
Withycombe Barn
Withycombe
B 3223
Spr
North Ley
South Ley
Edgcott
Kennels
H Ram
Thorne
Sprs
340
372
360
300
Pennycombe Water
337
Sellbed Cross
Sprs
Chibbet Post
Chibbet Hill
W
328
320
300
340
354
286
Chibbet
Chibbet Ford
Spr
350
290
Buckworthy
W
Buckworthy Plantation
83
84
85
370
Pennycombe Wood
359
Higher Blackland Farm
Blackland Iron Mine (disused)
Adit
Shaft (dis)
Halsgrove Farm
370
Lower Blackland Farm
Spr
Blackland Woods
Sparrow Lane
350
330
Hillway
Kitridge
H Ram
Spr
Kitridge Lane
349
260
Leys
310
Weather
Foxtwitchen
Spr
Newland Wood
330
FB
Brightworthy
Strong Ford
300
Newland House
270
Newland
Spr
Knighton
260
280
Newland Ford
310
330
350
Combe Gate Ford
Waterhouse Farm
257
Withypool
Resr
Mill Bridge
P
PO
Cattle Grid
King's Farm
Newhouse
Spr
South Hill
Fords

Simonsbath to Lynmouth
Start: Simonsbath
Finish: Lynmouth
Distance: 17.5km (11 miles)
EXMOOR
392
390
380
370
376
B 3223
Ashcombe
Plantation
326 Simonsbath
Wins
C
SF
B 3358
Simonsbath
Bridge
Birchcleave
380
River Barle
Two Moors Way
350
ttle Cornham
Cornham Brake
Halscombe
Plantation
Mount
Pleasant
367
Halscombe
330
Drybridge Combe
350
Exmoor
390
310
400
Little Halscombe
33
Flext
Memorial
425
Deer Park
442.
454
Blue
Gate
ulus
450
440
432
430
420
413
Wintershead
Farm
410
402
410
400
Kinsford Water
Ford
350
340
76
77
78
435
420
430
400
370
310
G

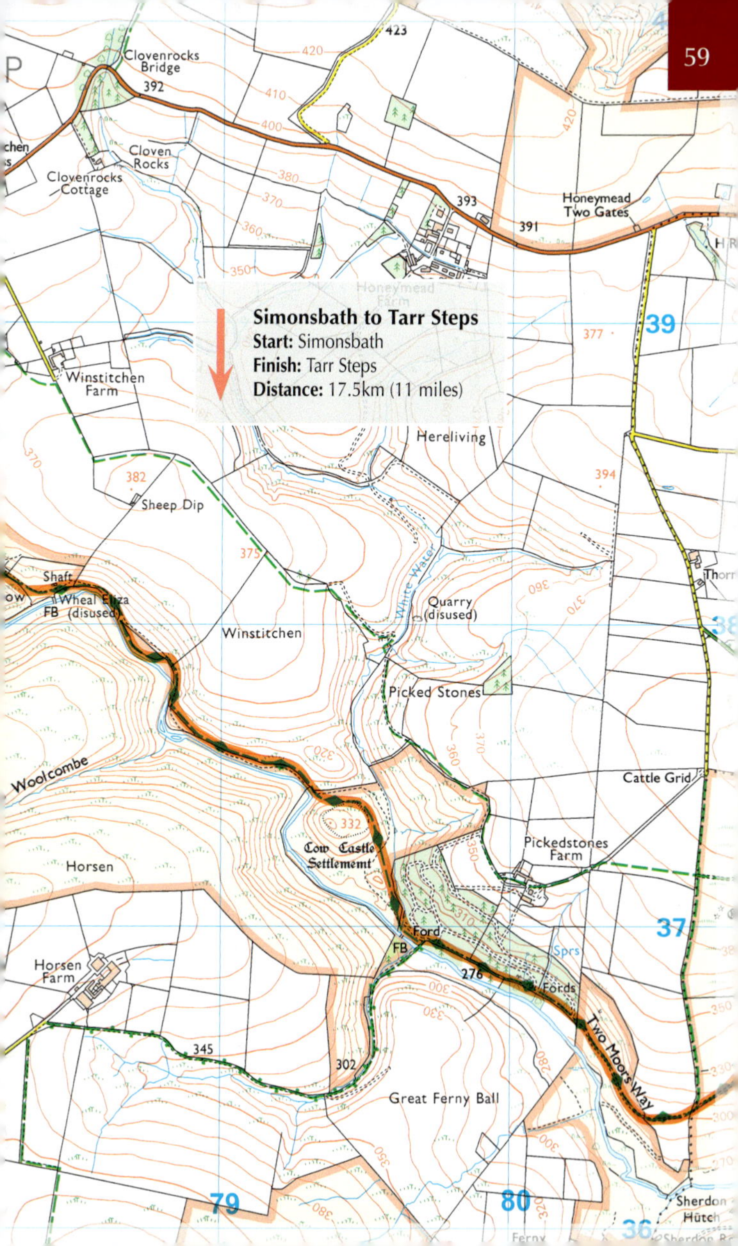
Clovenrocks Bridge
392
Cloven Rocks
Clovenrocks Cottage
423
420
410
400
380
370
360
350
393
391
Honeymead Two Gates
39
Winstitchen Farm
370
Hereliving
394
377
Sheep Dip
382
375
White Water
Quarry (disused)
360
370
Thorn
38
Shaft
Wheal Eliza
FB (disused)
Winstitchen
Picked Stones
Woolcombe
320
360
370
Cattle Grid
332
Cow Castle Settlememt
350
Pickedstones Farm
37
Horsen
310
Horsen Farm
Ford
FB
Sprs
276
Fords
345
302
330
300
280
Two Moors Way
350
Great Ferny Ball
79
80
300
320
36
Sherdon Hutch
Ferny
Sherdon

Simonsbath to Tarr Steps
Start: Simonsbath
Finish: Tarr Steps
Distance: 17.5km (11 miles)

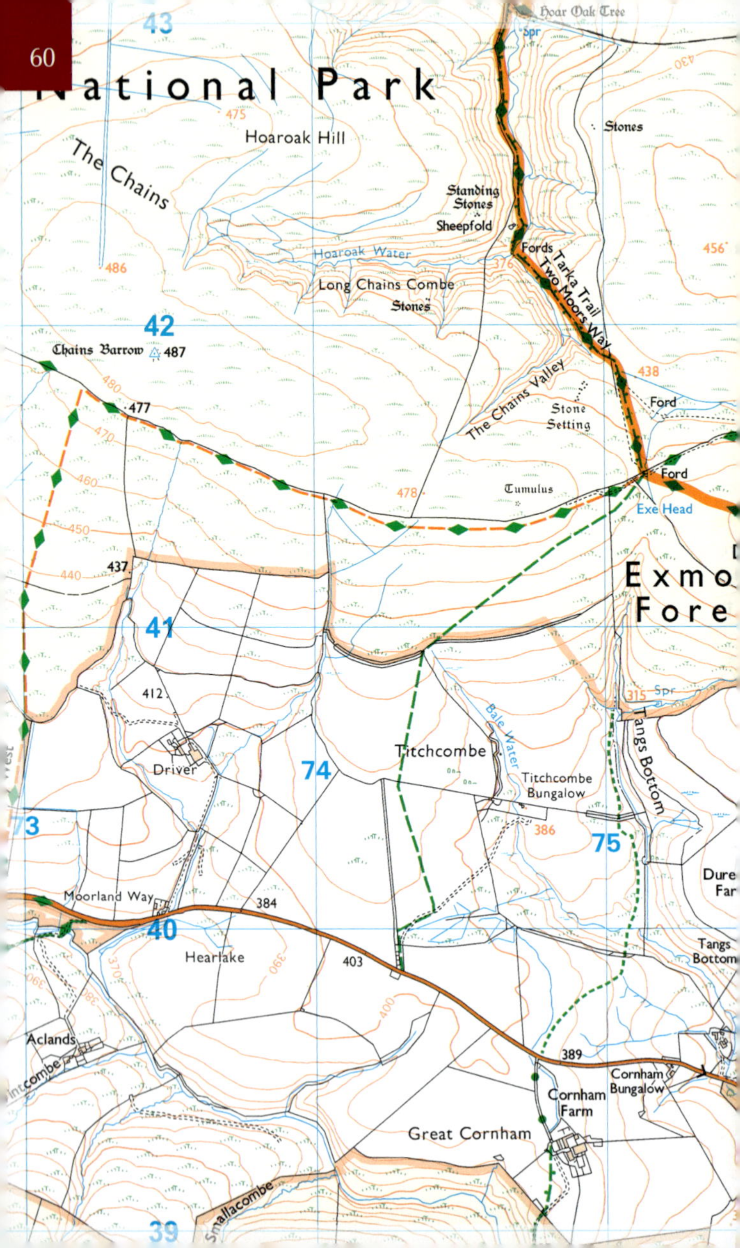

60
43
National Park
The Chains
Hoaroak Hill
475
486
Chains Barrow 487
42
480
477
470
460
450
440
437
41
412
Driver
73
Moorland Way
40
384
Hearlake
390
370
380
390
Aclands
lincombe
Smallacombe
39
Hoaroak Water
Long Chains Combe
Stones
478
Standing Stones
Sheepfold
Stones
Hoar Oak Tree
Spr
Stones
456
Fords
Tarka Trail
Two Moors Way
The Chains Valley
Stone Setting
438
Ford
Ford
Exe Head
Tumulus
Exmo
Fore
315
Spr
Tangs Bottom
Titchcombe
Bale Water
Titchcombe Bungalow
386
75
Dure Far
Tangs Bottom
74
403
400
389
Cornham Bungalow
Cornham Farm
Great Cornham
430
376

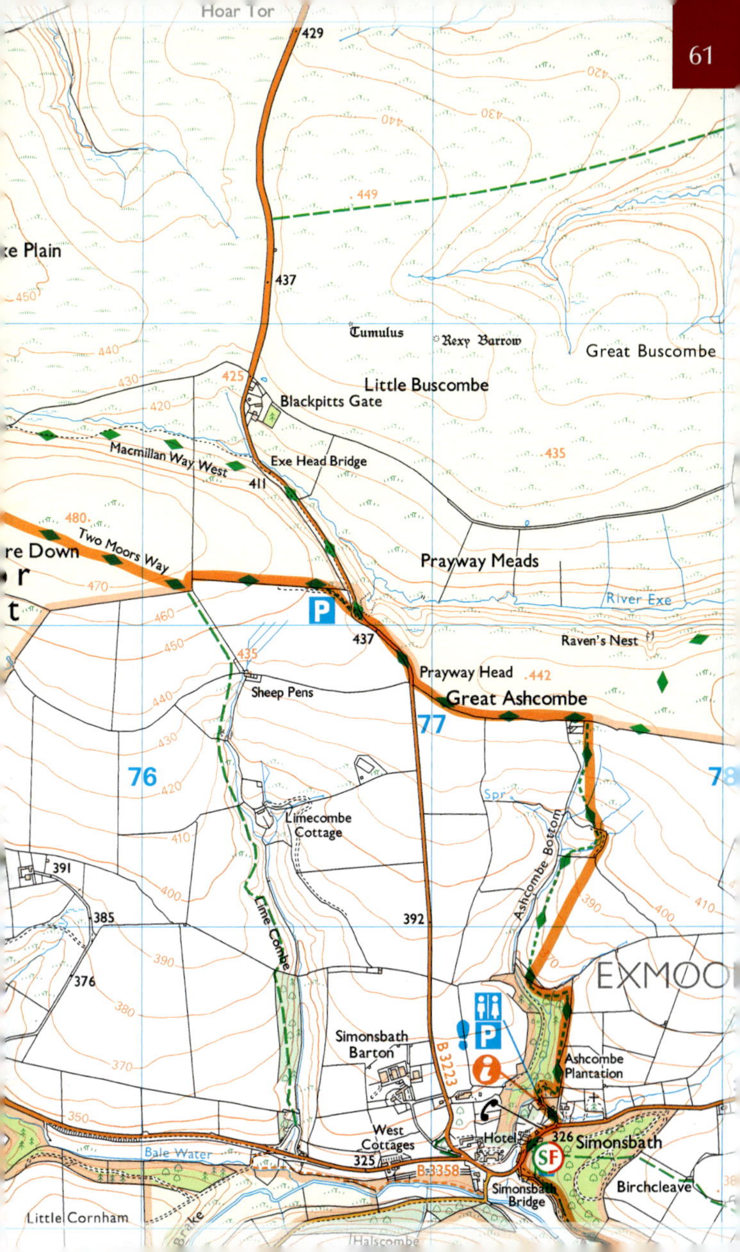
Hoar Tor
429
61
Plain
437
440
430
449
420
Tumulus
Rexy Barrow
Great Buscombe
Little Buscombe
440
425
Blackpitts Gate
430
420
435
Macmillan Way West
Exe Head Bridge
411
480
Two Moors Way
re Down
r
t
470
Prayway Meads
River Exe
460
450
Raven's Nest
435
437
450
Prayway Head
442
Sheep Pens
Great Ashcombe
440
77
430
76
420
78
410
Limecombe
Cottage
Ashcombe Bottom
Spr
390
391
400
410
Lime Combe
385
392
390
400
376
380
EXMOO
370
Simonsbath
Barton
Ashcombe
Plantation
350
B 3223
West
Cottages
Hotel
326 Simonsbath
Bale Water
325
SF
B 3358
Little Cornham
Simonsbath
Bridge
Birchcleave
Brake
Halscombe

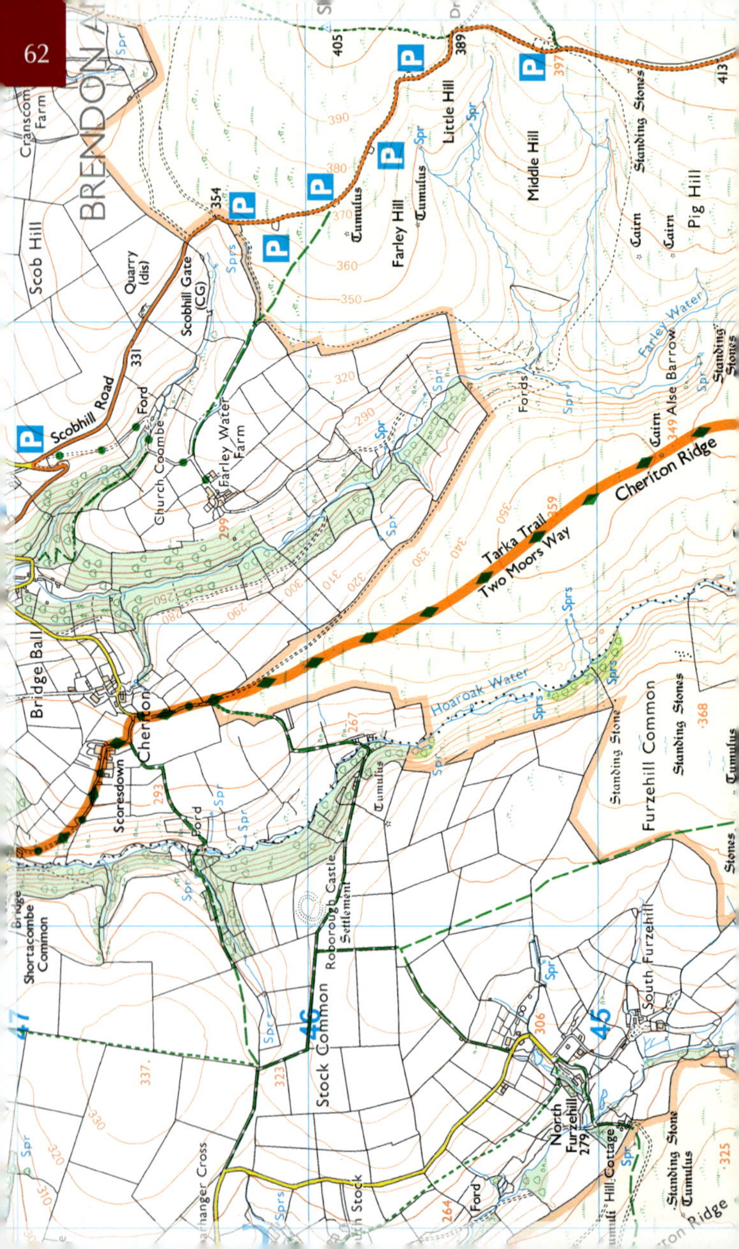
BRENDON A
Cranscombe Farm
Scob Hill
Scobhill Road
Quarry (dis)
Scobhill Gate (CG)
354
331
Ford
Church Coombe
Farley Water Farm
299
Bridge Ball
Bridge
Shortacombe Common
Cheriton
Scoresdown
293
Ford
390
380
370
360
350
405
Tumulus
Farley Hill
Little Hill
389
Middle Hill
397
Pig Hill
413
Tumulus
320
290
310
320
300
290
280
270
250
260
340
330
Spr
Spr
Spr
Spr
Spr
Spr
Spr
Spr
Spr
Sprs
Fords
Farley Water
Standing Stones
Cairn
Cairn
Cairn
349 Alse Barrow
Standing Stones
Cairn
Cheriton Ridge
Tarka Trail
Two Moors Way
259
350
267
Hoaroak Water
Sprs
Sprs
Sprs
Spr
Spr
Standing Stone
Furzehill Common
Standing Stones
368
Stones
Standing Stone
Roborough Castle Settlement
Tumulus
Tumulus
Stock Common
46
47
45
337.
323
330
320
310
Spr
Spr
Spr
Spr
Sprs
Sprs
Spr
Spr
306
North Furzehill
279
Hill Cottage
South Furzehill
Standing Stone
Tumulus
325
264
Ford
Tumuli
Ridge
harhanger Cross
ch Stock

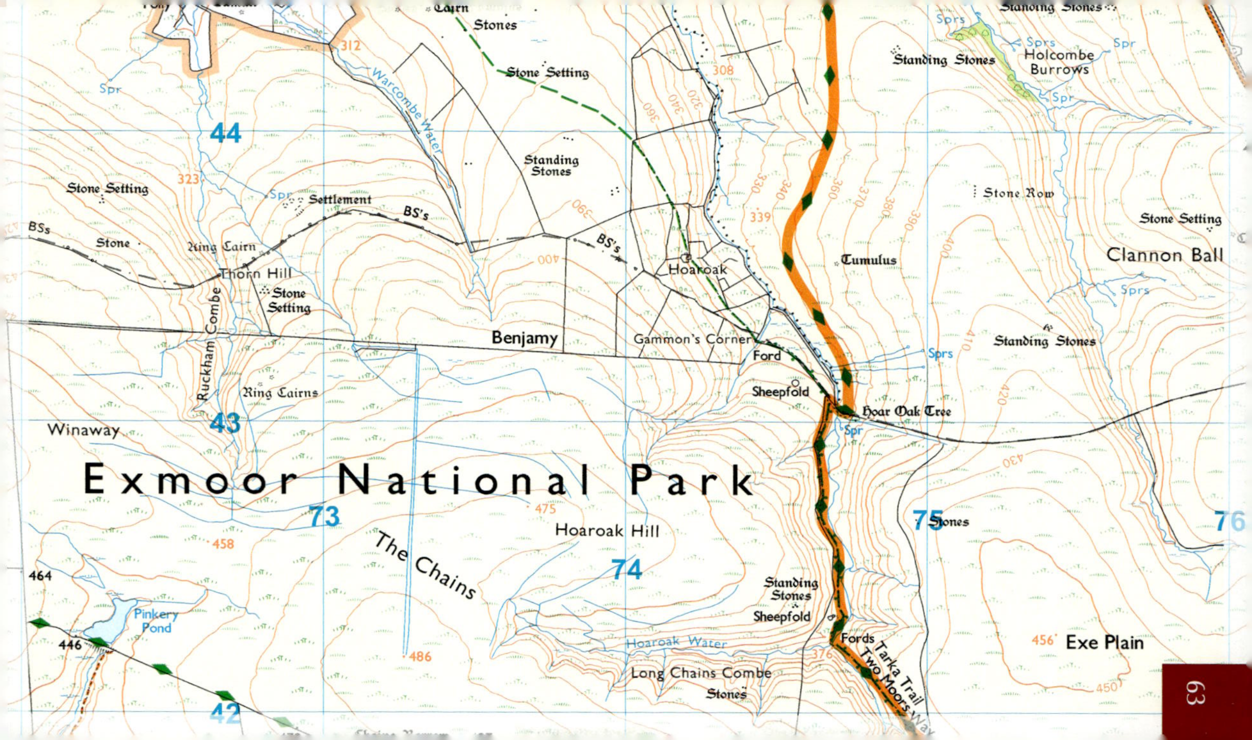
Exmoor National Park
Clannon Ball
Exe Plain
Holcombe Burrows
Standing Stones
Standing Stones
Standing Stones
Stone Row
Stone Setting
Sprs
Sprs
Sprs
Sprs
Sprs
Stone Setting
Stone
Settlement
BS's
BS's
Standing Stones
Thorn Hill
Ring Cairn
Ruckham Combe
Benjamy
Hoaroak
Gammon's Corner
Ford
Sheepfold
Tumulus
Hoar Oak Tree
Standing Stones
Sheepfold
Fords
Tarka Trail
Two Moors Way
Standing Stones
Winaway
Ring Cairns
Hoaroak Hill
The Chains
Pinkery Pond
Hoaroak Water
Long Chains Combe
Stones
Stones
BSs
44
43
73
74
75
76
42
312
323
308
339
360
340
320
330
370
380
390
400
410
420
430
450
456
458
464
475
486
446
376
Spr
Warcombe Water
Stone Setting
Cairn
Stones

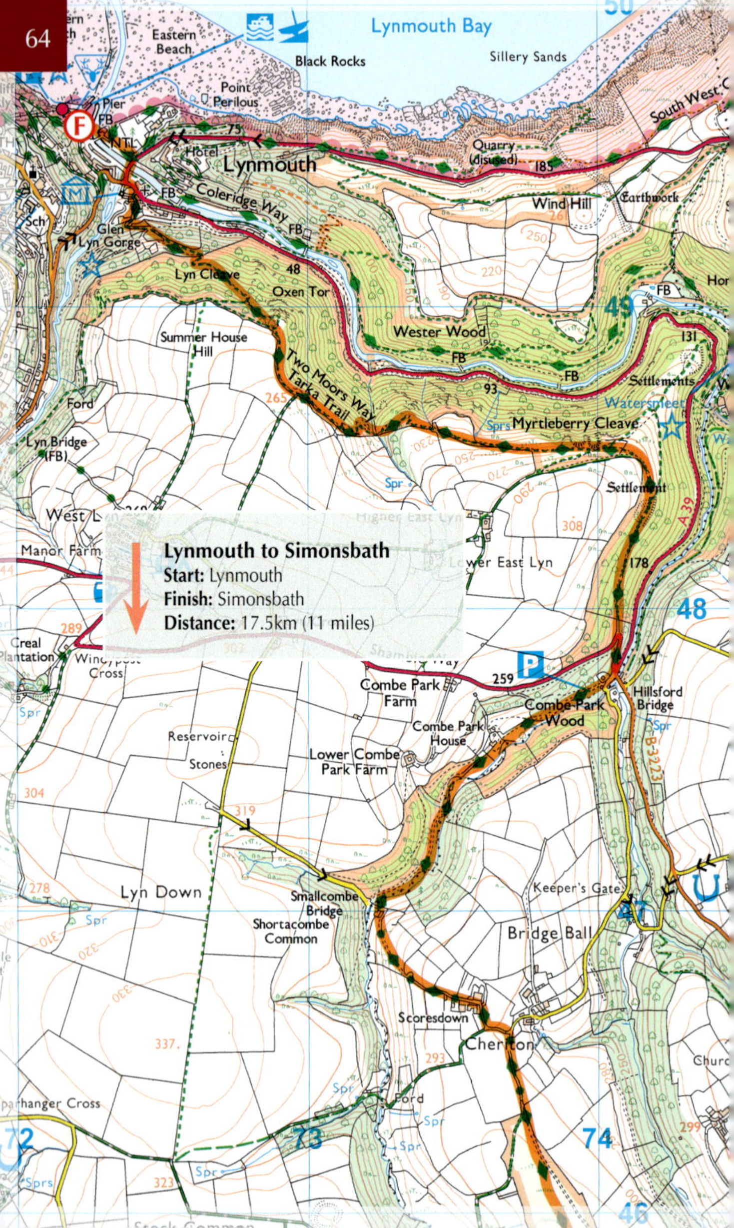

Lynmouth to Simonsbath
Start: Lynmouth
Finish: Simonsbath
Distance: 17.5km (11 miles)

LEGEND OF SYMBOLS
USED ON ORDNANCE SURVEY
1:25,000 (EXPLORER) MAPPING

ROADS AND PATHS — Not necessarily rights of way

M1 or A6(M)   Motorway   S Service Area   7 Junction Number

A 35   Dual carriageway

A30   Main road   S Service Area   T1 Toll road junction

B 3074   Secondary road

Narrow road with passing places

Road under construction

Road generally more than 4 m wide

Road generally less than 4 m wide

Other road, drive or track, fenced and unfenced

Gradient: steeper than 20% (1 in 5); 14% (1 in 7) to 20% (1 in 5)

Ferry   Ferry; Ferry P – passenger only

Path

RAILWAYS

Multiple track} standard
Single track } gauge

Narrow gauge or
Light rapid transit system
(LRTS) and station

Road over; road under; level crossing

Cutting; tunnel; embankment

Station, open to passengers; siding

PUBLIC RIGHTS OF WAY

Footpath

Bridleway

Byway open to all traffic

Restricted byway

The representation on this map of any other road, track or path is no evidence of the existence of a right of way

ARCHAEOLOGICAL AND HISTORICAL INFORMATION

Site of antiquity   VILLA Roman   Visible earthwork

1066 Site of battle (with date)   Castle Non-Roman

Information provided by English Heritage for England and the Royal Commissions
on the Ancient and Historical Monuments for Scotland and Wales

OTHER PUBLIC ACCESS

Other routes with public access — The exact nature of the rights on these routes and the existence of any restrictions may be checked with the local highway authority. Alignments are based on the best information available

Recreational route

 National Trail  Long Distance Route

Permissive footpath / Footpaths and bridleways along which landowners have permitted public use but which are not rights of way. The agreement may be withdrawn
Permissive bridleway

Traffic-free cycle route

National cycle network route number – traffic free; on road

ACCESS LAND

DANGER AREA — Firing and test ranges in the area. Danger! Observe warning notices

MANAGED ACCESS — Access permitted within managed controls, for example, local byelaws. Visit **www.access.mod.uk** for information

England and Wales

Access land boundary and tint

Access land in wooded area

 Access information point

Portrayal of access land on this map is intended as a guide to land which is normally available for access on foot, for example access land created under the Countryside and Rights of Way Act 2000, and land managed by the National Trust, Forestry Commission and Woodland Trust. Access for other activities may also exist. Some restrictions will apply; some land will be excluded from open access rights. The depiction of rights of access does not imply or express any warranty as to its accuracy or completeness. Observe local signs and follow the Countryside Code.
Visit **www.countrysideaccess.gov.uk** for up-to-date information

BOUNDARIES

— + — + National

— · — · — County (England)

— — — — Unitary Authority (UA), Metropolitan District (Met Dist), London Borough (LB) or District

(Scotland & Wales are solely Unitary Authorities)

· · · · · · · · · · Civil Parish (CP) (England) or Community (C) (Wales)

National Park boundary

VEGETATION

Limits of vegetation are defined by positioning of symbols

Coniferous trees

Non-coniferous trees

Coppice

Orchard

Scrub

Bracken, heath or rough grassland

Marsh, reeds or saltings

HEIGHTS AND NATURAL FEATURES

52 · Ground survey height
284 · Air survey height

Surface heights are to the nearest metre above mean sea level. Where two heights are shown, the first height is to the base of the triangulation pillar and the second (in brackets) to the highest natural point of the hill

HEIGHTS AND NATURAL FEATURES

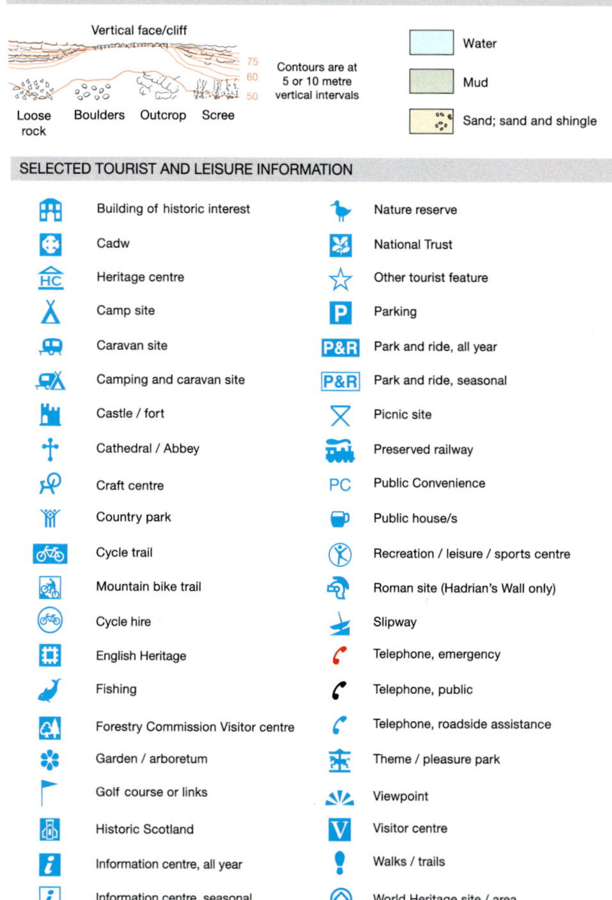

SELECTED TOURIST AND LEISURE INFORMATION

Building of historic interest	Nature reserve
Cadw	National Trust
Heritage centre	Other tourist feature
Camp site	Parking
Caravan site	Park and ride, all year
Camping and caravan site	Park and ride, seasonal
Castle / fort	Picnic site
Cathedral / Abbey	Preserved railway
Craft centre	Public Convenience
Country park	Public house/s
Cycle trail	Recreation / leisure / sports centre
Mountain bike trail	Roman site (Hadrian's Wall only)
Cycle hire	Slipway
English Heritage	Telephone, emergency
Fishing	Telephone, public
Forestry Commission Visitor centre	Telephone, roadside assistance
Garden / arboretum	Theme / pleasure park
Golf course or links	Viewpoint
Historic Scotland	Visitor centre
Information centre, all year	Walks / trails
Information centre, seasonal	World Heritage site / area
Horse riding	Water activites
Museum	Boat trips
National Park Visitor Centre (park logo) e.g. Yorkshire Dales	Boat hire

(For complete legend and symbols, see any OS Explorer map.)

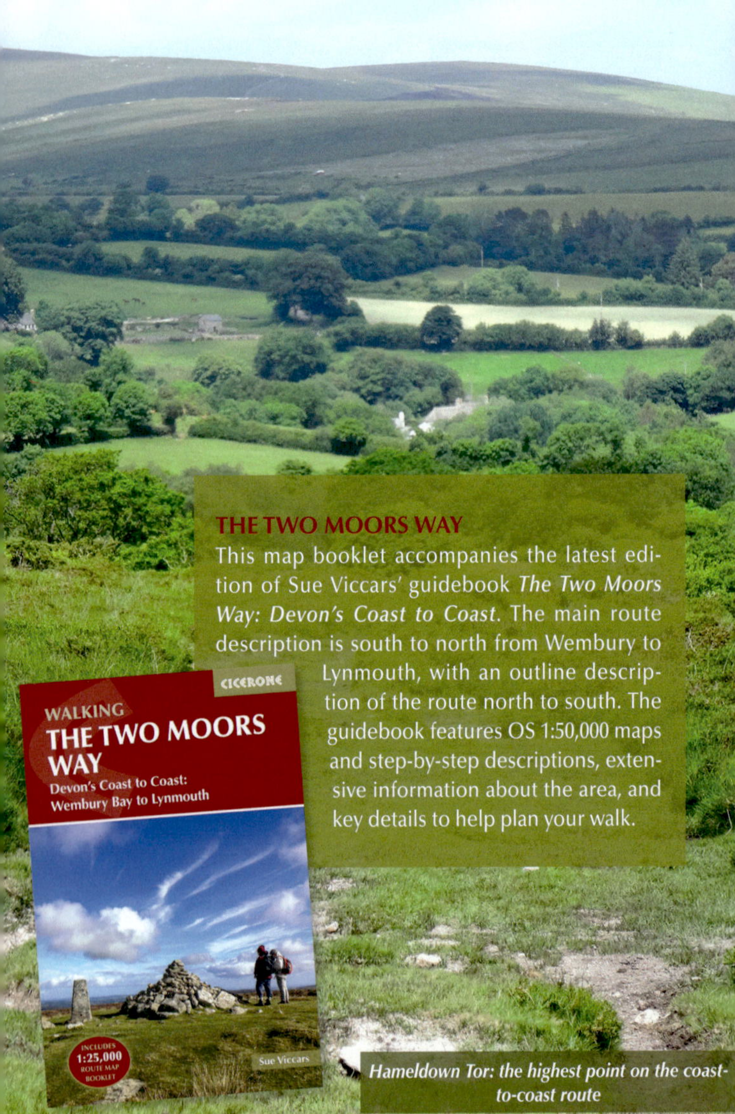

THE TWO MOORS WAY

This map booklet accompanies the latest edition of Sue Viccars' guidebook *The Two Moors Way: Devon's Coast to Coast*. The main route description is south to north from Wembury to Lynmouth, with an outline description of the route north to south. The guidebook features OS 1:50,000 maps and step-by-step descriptions, extensive information about the area, and key details to help plan your walk.

Hameldown Tor: the highest point on the coast-to-coast route

ROUTE SUMMARY TABLE

	Start	Finish	Distance	Time
1	Wembury Beach (SX 517 485)	Yealmpton (SX 579 518)	12km (7.5 miles)	4hr
2	Yealmpton (SX 579 518)	Ivybridge (SX 637 562)	14.5km (9 miles)	4hr 30min
3	Ivybridge (SX 637 562)	Holne (SX 706 695)	21.8km (13.5 miles)	7hr
3A	Ivybridge (SX 637 562)	Holne (SX 706 695)	26.8km (16.5 miles)	7hr 30min
4	Holne (SX 706 695)	Dunstone Down (SX 704 759); or Widecombe-in-the-Moor (SX 718 768)	11.5km (7.3 miles); or 14.5km (9 miles)	4hr; or 4hr 30min
5	Dunstone Down (SX 704 759); or Widecombe-in-the-Moor (SX 718 768)	Chagford Bridge (SX 694 880)	16.8km (10.5 miles)	5hr 30min
5A	Dunstone Down (SX 704 759); or Widecombe-in-the-Moor (SX 718 768)	Chagford Bridge (SX 694 880)	17.5km (11 miles)	6hr
6	Chagford Bridge (SX 694 880)	A377 south of Morchard Road (SS 756 043)	28.9km (18 miles)	8hr
7	A377 south of Morchard Road (SS 756 043)	Witheridge (SS 803 145)	16.8km (10.5 miles)	5hr 30min
8	Witheridge (SS 803 145)	Knowstone (SS 828 231)	12.5km (7.8 miles)	4hr
9	Knowstone (SS 828 231)	Tarr Steps (SS 868 361)	17.5km (11 miles)	5hr 15min
10	Tarr Steps (SS 868 361)	Simonsbath (SS 774 394)	17.5km (11 miles)	6hr
11	Simonsbath (SS 774 394)	Lynmouth, The Pavilion on The Esplanade (SS 723 497)	17.5km (11 miles)	6hr

NOTES

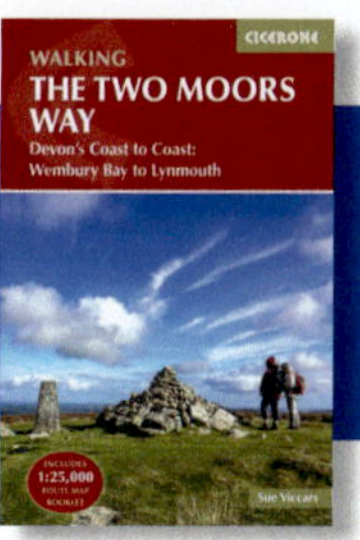

Other long distance guides

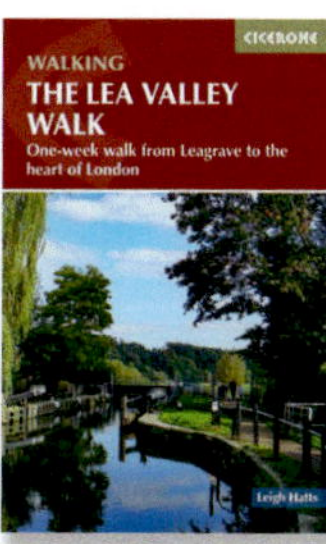

Other guides to this region

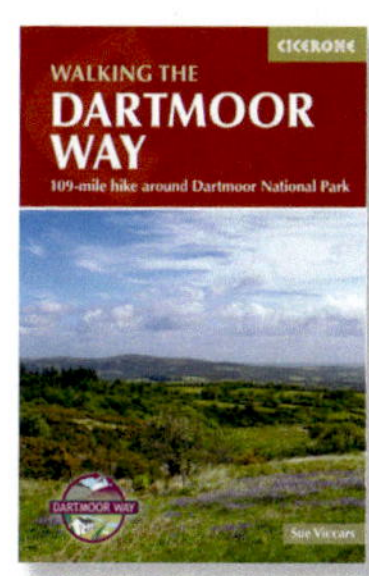

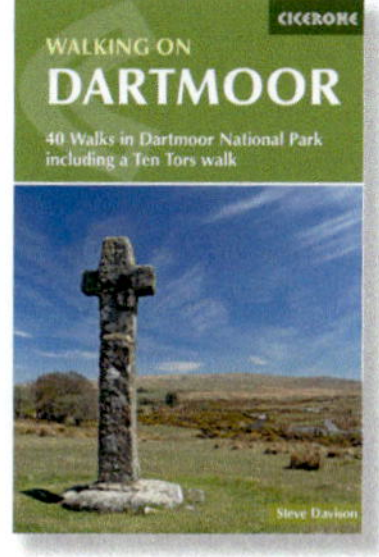

Trust Cicerone to guide your next adventure

cicerone.co.uk

Cicerone's gold-standard guides, now digital

Expert-curated routes

Follow routes crafted by expert authors who know each area inside out.

Plan with confidence

Find detailed facilities information and discover local landmarks along the way.

Download GPS-enabled maps

Navigate confidently wherever you are, even without a signal.

Discover more adventures in our expanding collection at

cicerone.co.uk

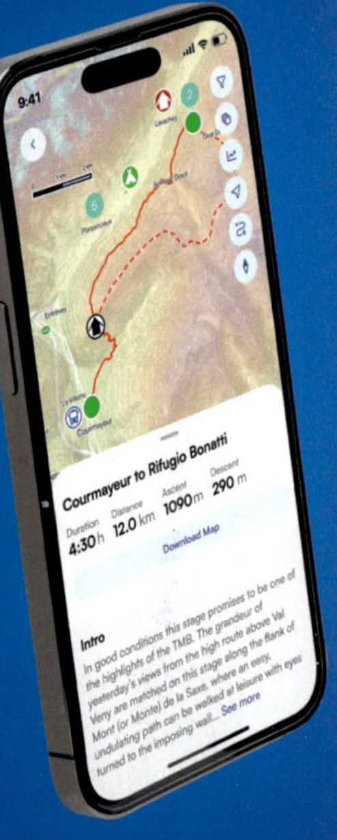